Engaging
Anabaptism

Engaging Anabaptism

Conversations with a Radical Tradition

John D. Roth, Editor

Herald
Press

Scottdale, Pennsylvania
Waterloo, Ontario

Library of Congress Cataloging-in-Publication Data
Engaging Anabaptism : conversations with a radical tradition / John D.
Roth, editor.
    p. cm.
Includes bibliographical references and index.
ISBN 0-8361-9191-9 (alk. paper)
    1. Mennonites—Doctrines. 2. Anabaptists—-Doctrines.   I. Roth, John
    D., 1960-
    BX8122 .E54 2001
    284'.3--dc21
    2001004480

The paper used in this publication is recycled and meets the minimum
requirements of American National Standard for Information Sciences—
Permanence of Paper for Printed Library Materials, ANSI Z39.48-1984.

Scripture is used by permission, with all rights reserved, and unless otherwise noted, is from the *New Revised Standard Version Bible,* copyright 1989
by the Division of Christian Education of the National Council of the
Churches of Christ in the USA.

ENGAGING ANABAPTISM
Copyright © 2001 by Herald Press, Scottdale, Pa. 15683
    Published simultaneously in Canada by Herald Press,
    Waterloo, Ont. N2L 6H7. All rights reserved
Library of Congress Catalog Card Number: 2001004480
International Standard Book Number: 0-8361-9191-9
Printed in the United States of America
Cover design by Gary Kauffman
Book design by Jim Butti

10 09 08 07 06 05 04 03 02 01   10 9 8 7 6 5 4 3 2 1

To order or request information, please call 1-800-759-4447 (individuals);
1-800-245-7894 (trade). Website: www.mph.org

Table of Contents

Contributors

James Wm. McClendon Jr. (1924-2000) was most recently Distinguished Scholar-in-Residence at Fuller Theological Seminary, Pasadena, California. He authored, among others, the influential titles *Ethics: Systemic Theology* (Abingdon 1988) and *Doctrine* (Abingdon 1994).

Stanley M. Hauerwas is the Gilbert T. Rowe Professor of Theological Ethics at Duke University and author of many books including *The Peaceable Kingdom: A Primer in Christian Ethics* (University of Notre Dame 1984), *Resident Aliens: A Life in the Christian Colony* (Abingdon 1989), and the recent *A Better Hope: Resources for a Church Confronting Capitalism, Democracy, and Postmodernity* (Brazos 2000).

Christopher Marshall is professor of New Testament at the Bible College of New Zealand. His newest book is *Christ and Crime: Biblical Foundations for a Christian Perspective on Justice, Crime and Punishment* (Eerdmans, forthcoming).

Nancey Murphy is Professor of Christian Philosophy at Fuller Theological Seminary, Pasadena, California. She is the author of *Beyond Liberalism and Fundamentalism: How Modern and Postmodern Philosophy Set the Theological Agenda* (Trinity Press 1996) and *Reconciling Theology and Science: A Radical Reformation Perspective* (Thorsons 1997).

Glen H. Stassen is Lewis B. Smedes Professor of Christian Ethics at Fuller Theological Seminary, Pasadena, California, and author of *Capital Punishment: A Reader* (Pilgrim Press 1998) and *Just Peacemaking: Ten Practices for Abolishing War* (Pilgrim Press 1998).

Samuel Escobar is the Thornley B. Wood Professor of Missiology at Eastern Baptist Theological Seminary, author of *Christian Mission and Social Justice* (Herald Press 1978), and editor of the journal *Missiology*.

Christopher Rowland is Dean Ireland's Professor of the Exegesis of Holy Scripture in the University of Oxford and a priest in the Church of England. He is the author of *Liberating Exegesis: The Challenge of Liberation Theology to Biblical Studies* (John Knox 1990) and *Revelation* (Epworth Commentaries, Trinity Press 1997).

Stuart Murray is Oasis Director of Church Planting and Evangelism at Spurgeon's College, London, England, co-author of the new release *Church Planting: Laying a Foundation* (Herald Press 2001), and editor of the British journal *Anabaptism Today*.

Eoin de Bhaldraithe is a Cistercian brother and abbot at Bolton Abbey, Moone, Ireland.

Richard J. Mouw is President and Professor of Christian Philosophy at Fuller Theological Seminary, Pasadena, California. His newest titles include *The Calvinistic Concept of Culture* (Baker Book House 2001) and *The Smell of Sawdust: What Evangelicals Can Learn from Their Fundamentalist Heritage* (Zondervan 2000).

Richard B. Hays is Professor of New Testament at The Divinity School, Duke University and author of *Echoes of Scripture in the Letters of Paul* (Yale University 1993) and *The Moral Vision of the New Testament: Community, Cross, New Creation: A Contemporary Introduction to New Testament Ethics* (Harper San Francisco 1996).

Rodney Clapp is cofounder and editorial director of Brazos Press in Grand Rapids, Michigan. He is author of several books including *A Peculiar People: The Church as Culture in a Post-Christian Society* (InterVarsity 1996).

Michael G. Cartwright is an ordained United Methodist minister appointed to serve as Associate Professor of Philosophy and Religion and Director of the Lantz Center for Christian Vocations at the University of Indianapolis. He co-authored with John Howard Yoder *The Royal Priesthood: Essays Ecclesiological and Ecumenical* (Herald Press 1994).

Editor's Preface

Ten years ago, *Christianity Today*—an evangelical journal not generally noted for its interest in sectarian or pacifist traditions—featured an essay by Charles Scriven with the eye-catching title "The Reformation Radicals Ride Again." After nearly four-and-a-half centuries of public indifference, misrepresentation or ridicule, Scriven argued, Anabaptist theology was not only gaining a hearing among scholars but actually winning the admiration and respect of many mainstream evangelicals. In the decade since, Scriven's claim seems to have been amply borne out. Today Anabaptist-Mennonite theological themes, like the Old Order Amish, are almost chic—the inspiration for numerous books, scholarly conferences, and much high-minded debate.

This dramatic shift in public attitudes toward the Anabaptist-Mennonite tradition did not happen suddenly. The groundwork was laid in the aftermath of World War II by the practical witness of scores of relief and service volunteers, and by an emerging openness among Protestants, especially in war-torn Europe, to engage conversations about Christian social responsibility and pacifism. At the same time, a generation of influential American scholars teaching at prestigious universities—people like Franklin Littell, Roland Bainton, and George Huntston Williams—helped to established the "Radical Reformation" as a field of respectable academic inquiry. In the broader culture, the Cold War and ensuing nuclear arms race gave fresh relevance and urgency to Anabaptist concerns for peacemaking and reconciliation; and the secularizing impulses of post-Christian, postmodern Western culture have compelled virtually all Protestant denominations to reconceive themselves as voluntary or believers churches.

Against the backdrop of these broader transformations looms the towering intellectual figure of John Howard Yoder, the Mennonite theologian whose 1972 book *The Politics of Jesus* has established itself as the classic apologetic for Anabaptist ethics and ecclesiology. Until his death in 1997, Yoder worked tirelessly to articulate a believers church theology of peacemaking, reconciliation, and mutuality to an audience beyond the cultural and ethnic boundaries of the Mennonite community. During the last half of the twentieth century he—along with others such as Alan and Eleanor Kreider in England or Joe Leichty in Ireland—patiently nurtured conversations with a growing ecumenical network of church leaders and scholars around the themes of Anabaptist hermeneutics, ethics, and ecclesiology.

This collection of essays offers one attempt to take stock of that conversation in progress. In my role as editor of *The Mennonite Quarterly Review*, I invited sixteen scholars from a variety of denominational perspectives to reflect on how their theological or ethical understandings have been shaped by an engagement with the Anabaptist tradition. The invitation was cast quite generally, but I encouraged contributors to respond in both autobiographical as well as analytical terms. I also asked each scholar not to flinch from offering a critique of Anabaptist theology, highlighting what they considered to be its weakest aspects. The result of that invitation is the gathering of stories, reflections, and critical engagement that followed in the October 2000 issue of *The Mennonite Quarterly Review* and now, in this book.

Each of the thirteen essays included here is framed in a distinctive and often highly personal context, yet the mosaic that emerges does have a discernible pattern. Not surprisingly, nearly all the contributors note, usually with gratitude, the significant influence of John Howard Yoder in their initial exposure to Anabaptist theology. Nearly all cite with appreciation the distinctive emphases of the Anabaptist-Mennonite tradition: a New Testament hermeneutic, the Christocentric approach to ethics, the peace witness, the practice of mutual aid, the noncoercive epistemology, and a view of the church as an alternative, socially visible community. And nearly all express concern about the legalistic tendencies within the Anabaptist theological and ethical tradition. For many, especially those from more liturgical traditions, the absence of a sacramental theology within Anabaptism leaves its adherents susceptible to a works-righteousness that allows the divine initiative to be overshadowed by human efforts.

These concerns notwithstanding, readers eager to hear voices of praise for the Anabaptist-Mennonite witness will find plenty to savor in this book. Yet such praise is clearly a double-edged sword. On one hand, admiration from quarters that had once relegated Anabaptism to the scrap heap of theological history is a rather heady experience, evoking sentiments ranging from quiet gratitude to smug self-satisfaction. At the same time, however, the sectarian impulse to self-conscious hand-wringing, especially in the face of encomiums, is never far from the surface. Is such praise really merited? Are the essayists aware of the yawning gap between Anabaptist ecclesiology and the lived reality of many contemporary Mennonite congregations? Or in a slightly different vein, will the growing public affirmation of the Anabaptist tradition inevitably blunt its radical edge? Can one embrace Anabaptist-Mennonite themes of pacifism without a corporate memory of suffering? Does the growing impulse to frame Anabaptist-Mennonite theology in the systematic, highly self-conscious language of the academy inevitably attenuate a faith that is best expressed in daily discipleship and the lived experience of the community? Such questions and dozens more ensure that the conversation will continue.

—*John D. Roth*
Goshen, Indiana
March 2001

CHAPTER ONE

The Radical Road
One Baptist Took

James Wm. McClendon Jr.

I was born in Shreveport, Louisiana, in 1924, the son of a
Methodist father and a Baptist mother. My parents faithfully attended their respective churches, but motherhood
being what it is, I was usually taken along to the Baptist
Sunday school and church. The church building was beautiful, echoing the Byzantine style, and the services as I now
recall them were stately and serious. Throughout my youth
the pastor was a man of considerable liturgical skill, a widely known denominational leader, and also a leader in a
Baptist version of ecumenism both in Shreveport and
beyond. He made round-the-world trips, preaching and baptizing on all the continents of the earth. I admired him. In my
tenth or eleventh year I was inwardly persuaded that faith in
Jesus was the way for me. I presented myself to the church in
the customary manner and was immersed in the "Byzantine"
church baptistry—an event still powerful in my memory. The
reading of the Bible (King James Version), attendance at
morning and evening Sunday services, and home prayers, at
least before every meal, were a part of the discipline that surrounded me as I grew through the school years. So was
enrolling in the high school Junior ROTC—a step I took as a
matter of course, yet without displaying any noteworthy military talents.

The Experience of War

American entry into World War II came while I was a college freshman. The question that the Pearl Harbor attack raised for American Christian youths like me was not whether to enlist in the armed forces of our country, but in which service to enlist. The churches' (and my parents') attitude to war was that it was a necessary evil in an evil world—which seemed a view common to most people around me throughout my college and even seminary years. Pacifism was not an issue in the South that I knew. None of the Baptist churches I belonged to made any pretense of opposing war as such, nor did the teachers in the Baptist and Presbyterian schools I attended. I enrolled in the Naval Reserve during my second college year, but the Navy, after calling me to active duty in the summer of 1943, sent me back to school. By the time the war with Hitler's Germany had ended, I had been commissioned an Ensign, USNR, and had graduated from Navy electronics schools at Harvard and MIT. Soon I had orders to report for duty as electronics officer aboard a ship I was to meet in Pearl Harbor: an "attack transport," *The Herald of the Morning*, AP 173. On the day I went aboard my ship in 1945, the peace treaty ending World War II was signed in Tokyo Bay, prompting a McClendon family joke that when Japanese intelligence learned I was now aboard ship, they just gave up. Though my ship had been fitted with small boats to transport troops to assault enemy beaches, her post-combat assignment, starting about the time I came aboard, was to be a troop transport, bringing home Americans stationed across the Pacific: from Hawaii, the Philippines, and eventually Japan as well.

While I was still ashore in Honolulu, a Baptist former missionary to Japan had given me the name of the longtime secretary or executive of the Tokyo YMCA, Soichi Saito. This gentleman, I was told, spoke English and would probably welcome a visitor who was acquainted with some of his prewar American friends. So when my ship steamed into Tokyo Bay and berthed in Yokohama, I took a commuter train to

Tokyo, standing somewhat self-consciously in the aisle in my gray Navy uniform with its shoulder boards and stripes, tall among the shorter Japanese.

In Tokyo I found the YMCA, located in the historic Ginza district, and was indeed received by Saito, who spoke competent if unpracticed English. He promptly presented me with a welcome gift, a large Japanese persimmon, and offered me a knife with which to cut into it. The staff of the YMCA, mainly young women in kimonos, gathered in a circle around me, politely bowed, and waited for me to slice. What I did next is a matter that, more than fifty years later, I hesitate to report. Having been alerted by the ship's medical officer to the danger of eating raw fruit in strange lands, I awkwardly stammered to my Japanese hosts that I would take the persimmon back to the ship with me. What did not even occur to me was that in Japan, immediately after the war, persimmon might have been the only fruit my hosts had seen that day or any recent day. Quite conceivably, some of them were hungry that morning. Had I cut the persimmon and shared it with the watching staff, each might have had a bite—a little symbolic meal of peace. As it was, I left with their persimmon, maybe their only persimmon, bulging in my pocket.

But the main event was still to come. Mr. Saito took me, recent enemy, uniformed naval officer, on a walking tour of central Tokyo. Soon we came to a vast, cleared area, the site of the fire-bombing of the city during the preceding year. Fire-bombing, a tactic that made atom bombs redundant, had been developed in Europe as the most effective way to destroy cities. It involved creating a heat so intense that high winds rushed in to make an entire city a holocaust of unquenchable fire. When in the last stages of the war this technique was tried by the U.S. on densely residential Tokyo, fire-bombing scored another "success." Secretary Saito and I stood in an area where for many blocks in either direction one could see only paved streets and empty lots—much as in a new part of a city still unbuilt—in the heart of Tokyo's residential district. Here houses or apartments had stood close together. Here, a few months earlier, housewives had hung wash on lines. Here children had recently done homework and ridden tricycles and played hide-and-seek. But there had been no hiding in Tokyo the night of the fire. Saito located a small X seared into the asphalt of an empty street. Here, he said, one of the bombs had landed and begun its hot work.

I was young, I was callow, and I still had a youth's insensitive exterior. I had felt a certain awkwardness in accepting the persimmon, though I was not sure why—certainly not because of hungry staff members at the YMCA. I felt no awkwardness, though, in surveying the devastation my nation had caused in my war. So, I said to myself, this is war. I'm certainly glad our side won. Inwardly I shrugged. Outwardly I thanked my host for his interesting tour and went my way with the persimmon still innocently resting inside the flap pocket of my gray uniform.

This part of the story can be concluded quickly. In the 1950s and again in the 1960s, America made war again, this time in Southeast Asia: Vietnam, Laos, Cambodia. I was no pacifist, but by then I had become a politically concerned university professor at the (Jesuit) University of San Francisco. The faculty in which I taught needed some organizing, I thought, to help it oppose what I conceived in Niebuhrian fashion to be the wrong war at the wrong time in the wrong place. Soon I became the leader of a large faculty group opposing the war. We publicized a joint letter to President Lyndon Johnson urging him to withdraw from Vietnam. The university, not eager to have its patriotism questioned in the turbulent 1960s, soon thereafter asked me to resign my post, though my teaching evaluations from students had been the highest in the faculty. I was asked to go, and I left.

A couple of teaching appointments later, I found myself teaching a January session on the ethics of war and peace in an eastern college. There it dawned upon me that I had come to oppose not only Asian wars, not only unjust wars, but all wars. Perhaps I recalled Mr. Saito and fire-bomb-devastated

Tokyo. At the very least, I no longer believed that violence was an option for a Christian. Imperceptibly, without the splendor of a conversion, I had become some kind of pacifist! Yet I had done so without acquiring any grand theory of non-violence (I still lack one), without even the dignity of belonging to a "peace church" (I have some doubts about that category), and without learning very much about the broader peace movement (though I had attended Quaker meetings in Baltimore). I simply believed, by that January 1970 term, that war in our time was wrong. Wrong for me, and thus wrong for anyone like me; and—since I could heartily wish that all were like me in being followers of Jesus—at least potentially wrong for everyone the world round. Certainly it was wrong for my older son, who by that time had declared his conscientious objection to war to the local draft board, been rejected by their process, and was engaged in a struggle to claim his right to alternative service which was not easy for a youth whose only church connection was Baptist. I stood by my son Will and in doing so found my own convictions strengthened.

I tell this true story to show that I am not to be readily classed with this or that or the other set of pacifists. In my case a conviction grew, but not from a root in high pacifist theory, and not from training in a "peace church" ethos. That frees me, though, as others may not be free, to ask about the necessary connection here between Christian ethics and Christian doctrine. Is there a structure of Christian faith that, even though not explicit, had worked upon me, a teacher of ethics and doctrine, leading me to a conviction I had not expected, along paths I did not seek? I now believe there is.

Theological Consequences

My academic training in theology came first from Southwestern Baptist Theological Seminary in Fort Worth, which could rightly boast of its size if not of its high academic standards, then from Princeton Theological Seminary (somewhat more rigorous academically), and finally again from

Southwestern where I had hoped to finish a doctorate under a fine old systematician, Walter Thomas Conner. Unfortunately, he died and I was left to finish my doctoral work with little supervision—an outcome that may incidentally have raised my academic sights a bit. Left to myself, I concentrated on biblical theology and wrote a dissertation that, had I named it properly, might have been called "The Doctrine of Perfection in 1 John and Its Reflection in Modern Christianity."[1] Something biblical was at work in me but, at the same time, left to myself, I began to widen my exposure to ecumenical Christianity—to Eastern Orthodoxy and Catholicism, but especially to the wider Protestant heritage whose chief U.S. theologians in those days were such as the Niebuhr brothers and Paul Tillich. To my surprise, though, I found they had little to say about the "perfectionism" of 1 John and its heritage. Their work, closely examined, had clearly misunderstood it.

After a few years as a Louisiana Baptist pastor, in 1954 I accepted the invitation to teach at the Golden Gate (Southern) Baptist Seminary in the San Francisco area. During those years especially, I sought to widen my ecumenical bearings and connections. So when in 1966 I decided to leave GGBTS (partly on account of the tension growing out of the opposition to that Southeast Asian War already mentioned), I was blessed with non-Baptist friends who helped me find places to teach: Stanford for a visiting term, the University of San Francisco (where patriotism, I later learned, was not about to let itself be threatened), and briefly on the East Coast at Temple University, at Goucher College in Baltimore (where I taught the course on war and peace), and at the University of Pennsylvania, all for short visiting appointments. In time, I received a more permanent invitation to teach in the San Francisco Bay area where my family had remained, in the (Episcopal) Church Divinity School of the Pacific, which was part of the Graduate Theological Union, Berkeley, California. By this time I had gained possibly the widest-ranging teaching experience of any living

American theologian. The schools I had served were Southern Baptist, Roman Catholic (my appointment at the University of San Francisco was the first of its kind in the U.S.), secular, Episcopalian, and (in the case of the G.T.U.) ecumenically Christian.

Two circumstances shaped me theologically during the Church Divinity School years (1971-90). The first was that I found Episcopalians liked to say they were both Protestant and Catholic, yet I found the setting theologically uncomfortable. Why? Was the old Baptist claim that we were neither Protestant nor Catholic correct? Did our often-denied root in Anabaptism, the Radical Reformation, exist after all? My seminary teachers had scorned that connection. Baptists, they had assured me, were a variety of Reformed Protestants. Then why didn't I, as their graduate, fit comfortably into an environment rich in the Reformed (and Catholic) heritages?

The second circumstance seemed a mere happenstance. In 1967 I had briefly attended a "Believers Church" conference in Louisville, Kentucky (part of my determination to be ecumenical), and there had met young John Howard Yoder, one of its organizers. Later, in 1972, Yoder published *The Politics of Jesus*, and a year or two later I read it. That book changed my life. Implicit in it I found all the old awareness of being part of a Christianity somehow unlike the standard-account sort I had worked so hard to learn and to teach—yet somehow like what I had known as a youth growing up Baptist. Night and day I read through *Politics*, and by the time I had finished, I had undergone a second conversion. Not as at my baptism merely to follow Jesus, but now to follow Jesus understood this way. Jesus interpreted by John Yoder's scornful passion to overcome standard-account thinking, Jesus who (among other things) rejected the Zealot option, Jesus who would not do harm even in the best of causes, even in his own. By then, as I have said above, I had become some kind of anti-war Christian. I had stored in my memory something my friend Stanley Hauerwas once said to me in a telephone conversation—he in South Bend, I in Berkeley—that

John Yoder had persuaded him that violence was not an option for a Christian. "Isn't that just right?" I thought. I had opposed one war, even at the cost of my job. These persisting attitudes, my boyhood formation, and Yoder's relentless logic all converged; I was converted. I was—though I still have no love for the term itself—an "Anabaptist" Baptist.

The remainder of the story is easy to tell. Before long I had agreed with Daryl Schmidt, a Mennonite graduate student in New Testament in the G.T.U., to co-teach a seminar on the heritage of the Radical Reformation. We would start with the Sermon on the Mount (well within Daryl's academic competence). After that we would track the heritage from the sixteenth century to the present. The seminar was a big success—it attracted students, some of whom (e.g., Ched Myers, Nancey Murphy) have since made names for themselves in this kind of Christian thinking. I repeated the seminar in subsequent years, and have most recently taught it again at Fuller, where following Nancey (now my wife) I came to teach about a decade ago. In a few more teaching years after that radical conversion (in about 1980), I realized that I had to do what I thought no one else was doing: produce a systematic theology whose primary community of reference would not be Catholics or Protestants (or those who were somehow both) but heirs of Radical Reform.

That is easy to tell, but it has been hard to do. The book I envisioned would have three volumes. One on ethics (How must the church live now to really be the church?), one on doctrine (What must the church teach now to really be the church?), and a third one, taking the place of but not in any sense duplicating the usual "prolegomena" to systematic theology. The third and final volume, now called *Witness*, is due out in the year 2000, ending my two-decades task. But why has it been so hard to do, so slow to complete? Because I was determined to write every sentence in light of my new-gained radical convictions, and yet to write in such a way that standard-account people, those who shared my pre-Yoder standpoint, could make sense of it. And if not convinced (for who can say when God will work a conversion?), they could at least recognize that this, too, was a distinct, responsible Christian heritage that could not be subsumed under the other sorts. *Ethics* had to show why Christian conduct led on to peace, but without seeming dogmatic. *Doctrine* had to show how the risen Jesus Christ changed everything, made the world itself new, so that a Christian church, to be a Christian church, must center on Christ and, through him, on the God of peace. *Witness* had to show that we were not sectarians (in the pejorative sense), but that we had a theology of culture that could make sense of the whole world while inviting that world to find its way back to its own true center. The trilogy had to show that we were on the side of the world, even though we said "No" to its worldliness. In a way, for me, it was back to the doctoral dissertation of half a century before—to "perfection" and its perplexing demands.

Along the way, of course, there were other tasks. In the wake of the death-of-God movement I published a book about God, co-edited with Axel Steuer, now President of Gustavus Adolphus College in Minnesota.[2] With Nancey Murphy I co-authored an article about the shift from modernity to a new, post-modern way of philosophical work. Many theologians who had better educations than I were nevertheless taken by surprise by this shift and left in an intellectual backwater.[3] I co-edited a book with younger colleagues Curtis Freeman and Rosalee Velloso that tracked the theological texts from the fifteenth century (Petr Chelciky) to John Yoder himself, showing how "baptists" (my preferred label for this band of thinkers because the term points out to Baptists that maybe they are baptists!) had thought independently, yet in important ways, alike.[4] And I wrote other things as well, not least the book *Convictions*, with James M. Smith.[5] But the series of three volumes has been my work, my life, my strong demand for nearly twenty years.

One might conclude from these autobiographical recollections that I believe my own approach to radical reformation convictions and theology is normative for my students and colleagues. Assuredly I do not believe that. As this collection of essays makes evident, there are many approaches to this theology, and none of us is in a position to say, "Ours is best." We can only take a share in a very large task. I do look to my peers to provide an ethics that flowers into peacemaking: In Scripture's words, "Seek peace, and pursue it" (Ps. 34:14b KJV). It seems so far to be our special vocation among the followers of Jesus.

When it comes to doctrine, theology in this style has grown from at least three foci—experience, Scripture, and community. Examples of all three are easy to find, and they are not mutually exclusive. In the focus on "experience," those in the Radical Reformation tradition "taste and see that the Lord is good" (Ps. 34:8a KJV). Such experience properly focuses upon the love of God the Father—both God's love for us and our love for God. An early prototype is Hans Denck. When it comes to Scripture, the radical rule is to read it as the book of Christ—living, risen, lordly—whose costly way to his final triumph sets the tone for all radical reading strategies. Here a prototype is Michael Sattler, for whom Scripture is but a guide to the Way of Jesus. Community as a theological focus, if serious, demands a doctrine of the spirit. It is noteworthy that the Psalm just cited, like others, is addressed not to individuals but to a community of listeners. This solidarity in community is a proper third focus of Anabaptist theology. Prototypical is Menno himself, who shaped the churches according to his knowledge of the Spirit in the midst. Thus experience, Christ (witnessed in Scripture and alive), and community set the broad limits for our doctrinal task. But such limits are wide indeed, and an aim of this present essay has been to show, by one example, the variety of forms in which radical theology is shaped.

CHAPTER TWO

Confessions of a Mennonite Camp Follower

Stanley M. Hauerwas

Getting to Know You, Getting to Know All About You[1]

I am aware that I have a certain reputation among Mennonites. I felt honored that Craig Haas and Steve Nolt in their book *The Mennonite Starter Kit: A Handy Guide for the New Mennonite* included me in the list of "Non-Mennonites Whom Mennonites Wish Were Mennonites."[2] Since theirs is the most incisive book on contemporary Mennonite life, I clearly have been given a status I cannot pretend to deserve. It does give me pause, of course, that the list also includes Lloyd Bentsen (from Texas?), Rembrandt (catering no doubt to Mennonites' pretension that they care about art), Thomas Müntzer (they have to be kidding!), Ronald Reagan, and Alice Parker (who is Alice Parker?). So I am extremely pleased to have been asked to contribute this essay on how my "thought" has been shaped by an engagement with Radical Reformation theology.

My initial encounter with Mennonites did not go well. Growing up in Texas, I had never heard of the Mennonites. If I knew one or two, they did not make themselves known to me as Mennonites. I learned nothing about Mennonites at

Southwestern University in Georgetown, Texas. They may have been mentioned in some history or religion course, but I do not remember it. I must have read about Mennonites in Williston Walker's *A History of the Christian Church*, but whatever I read made no impression.[3] Only when I ran into actual Mennonites did I realize that there was something different about them—and I did not like the difference.

The first Mennonite I ever knew must have been Mel Schmidt, who appeared during my second or third year in seminary. He and his wife lived in married student housing, where we became acquainted. I vaguely remember that Mel withheld his taxes, or at least we had a discussion about tax withholding. Vietnam had not yet become the issue that made tax resistance the "thing to do." All I remember is that I thought it very strange that anyone would do anything that radical. Years later Mel and I crossed paths again, I lecturing and Mel a pastor in Bluffton, Ohio, and recalled my earlier stupidity.

However, the encounter with a Mennonite that I remember in more detail occurred in 1966 or 1967, during a trip to Harvard for a joint colloquium of Harvard and Yale graduate students in ethics. By this time the Vietnam war was the subject for endless discussions. In the car on the way to Cambridge we were debating whether or not the war was or was not just. In the course of the discussion a new and very quiet graduate student made statements that suggested he might be a pacifist. He even mentioned John Howard Yoder, of whom, of course, none of us had ever heard. I was shocked that the Yale Graduate School would actually accept anyone so naive. I, of course, tried to intimidate him, using Niebuhrian arguments. His name was Leroy Walters, and he is now the distinguished ethicist at the Kennedy Center for Bioethics at Georgetown University. Given Leroy's gentle demeanor, I suspect I got the better of the argument in the car on the way to Cambridge, but I hope Leroy finds some satisfaction in knowing that I now believe what he believed, even if he may have some uncertainties about what he once believed.

But at least Leroy (and the Vietnam war) had gotten my attention. I was busy, of course, writing about character and sanctification, so I did not think I had any reason to solve the ethical problems about war in general and the Vietnam war in particular. After all, I was a student at Yale, where we were taught to think critically about convictions even if we discovered we did not have any convictions of our own. Sometime during my last years at Yale, perhaps when I was finishing my dissertation, I was wandering through the Yale Divinity School Bookstore, which I did once a week or so in an effort to keep up on the "new stuff" coming out. My eye fell on a pamphlet entitled *Karl Barth and Christian Pacifism* by someone called John H. Yoder—by this time I had forgotten that Leroy had mentioned Yoder to me.[4] Since Barth played a major role in my dissertation, and the pamphlet cost only a dollar (the paper was cheap and the printing was just a step above mimeograph), I bought it.

I do not remember when I read Yoder's account of Barth's ethics, but I remember very clearly my reaction to Yoder's presentation of Barth. I thought, "That is the best critique of Barth's ethics I have ever read, but you would have to be crazy to accept Yoder's ecclesiology." He was, after all, a "sectarian." Even though Yoder's account and critique of Barth's understanding of the *Grenzfall* was analogous to the criticisms I had developed in my dissertation concerning Barth's occasionalism, I had no reason to think I should find out anything more about Yoder as I went to teach at Augustana College in Rock Island, Illinois. I thought that being a Methodist sanctificationist was enough of a challenge for the Lutherans at Augie.

Of course I managed to alienate the Lutherans, but I was rescued by the Catholics who hired me to teach at Notre Dame. What is important about Notre Dame, however, is that South Bend is close to Elkhart. Sometime during my first summer in South Bend, before I had begun teaching at Notre Dame, I thought it might be a good idea to get to know this Yoder. So I drove over to Goshen, assuming that he taught at

Goshen College. I discovered that that was not the case, but in the process I wandered into the College Mennonite Church, where I found a rack of pamphlets for twenty-five cents each. So I bought three that had been authored by Yoder: his earlier pamphlet on Barth, his essay on capital punishment, and one on Reinhold Niebuhr.

His criticisms of Reinhold Niebuhr were particularly important for me. I began to realize that I was not only reading the work of an extraordinarily powerful mind, but also that I could not have my account of the virtues and Reinhold Niebuhr too. Put differently, I began to understand that my "Barthianism," which is just another way of saying my Christology, was incompatible with Niebuhr's project to provide a theological justification of political realism. I had earlier begun to see the inadequacy of Niebuhr's understanding of political realism by reading political theorists such as William Connolly, Robert Paul Wolff, and Ted Lowi. But reading Yoder made me realize that I lacked an ecclesiology that could provide an alternative politics. I simply had to learn more about this Yoder guy.

Soon thereafter, I discovered a journal I did not know existed, *The Mennonite Quarterly Review*, by looking in the periodical index under Yoder's name and finding that he published in this journal. That was in 1970, so *The Original Revolution* had not been published. I think the first essays I read in *The Mennonite Quarterly Review* were "The Otherness of the Church" and "Peace Without Eschatology," both of which made an extraordinary impression on me.[5] I was all the more convinced that I had to get to know Yoder. I had somehow learned that Yoder was not at Goshen College, but taught at Elkhart. With my usual disregard for academic etiquette, I called John up and asked if I could come see him and he invited me over. Sometime that summer I barged into his office armed with a load of arrogance that only Yale can breed.

I do not remember much about that first encounter except that John was his usual diffident self and certainly did not try to charm me into agreeing with his work. Charm and Yoder are not exactly words that belong together. But I suppose the same might be said about me! John responded to my questions with his well known exactness, saying no more or less than needed to be said to answer what I am sure he thought were ill-formed queries. Because I did not yet know enough to really talk with John, I finally resorted to the academic game: "So what are you working on now?" He said, "Not anything very significant." He was mainly writing things for Mennonite audiences that would probably not interest me. He added that most of what he was doing remained unpublished.

I allowed (Texans "allow") that I was really interested in anything he was doing. So he went through his shelves and I left with a stack of papers about a foot high. I do not remember everything that was in that stack, but it did contain what we now know as *The Politics of Jesus*. I did not comprehend the significance of what I was reading, but I knew it was different. My problem was that I had been well enough educated at Yale to recognize what an extraordinary argument Yoder was making. I had taken a Christology course with Hans Frei in which we had studied not only the classical Christological debates and confessions, but also the work of some Protestant liberals. I had become, and remained, convinced that Chalcedon was and is normative for how we understand the full reality of Jesus as Israel's Messiah. But I was uneasy with Chalcedon insofar as so-called "high Christologies" threaten to make the life and teachings of Jesus secondary for Christian life and thought. So I read *The Politics of Jesus*, which Yoder claimed was merely a report on the consensus of New Testament scholarship, as an extraordinary Christological proposal.

I began to read everything of John's I could get my hands on. I was particularly impressed by *The Christian Witness to the State*, which I wanted to use in a course I had developed in response to the student rebellion, called Christianity, Ethics and Democratic Society. Discovering that it was out of print, I desperately called Faith & Life Press to see if I could get a hundred copies. In my first discovery of how community works in the Mennonite world, they were more than pleased to crank up the press to make sure I could get the copies I needed.

Although I was reading Yoder, I had still not decided that I could really endorse his project. Of course, he did not understand it to be his project. However, I felt I could not treat Yoder as representing merely one more position to fit into a Yale typology. Among the papers Yoder had given me was an early draft of his critique of H. Richard Niebuhr's *Christ and Culture*, an argument I found convincing. My chance to come to terms with Yoder came shortly thereafter when I was asked to do the paper for the yearly "ecumenical" meeting of the departments of theology at Valparaiso University and Notre Dame. I decided to write an essay pulling together what I had learned from Yoder.[6]

I began my presentation by noting that what I was going to do before these Lutherans and Catholics was a genuine ecumenical effort. It featured a Methodist with a doubtful theological background (if you are Methodist you have a doubtful theological background) representing a most Catholic department of theology, reading a paper to a group of Missouri Synod Lutherans and saying that the Anabaptists had been right all along. I said that it was an ecumenical gesture because, by the time I finished, the Catholics and Lutherans would discover how much they had in common—namely, thinking it a very good thing to kill the Anabaptists. And, of course, that is exactly what happened, as the Catholics and the Lutherans joined forces to try to show me why we should not take Yoder seriously. Serious people understand that sometimes you do need to kill somebody. I was not convinced, and the rest, so to speak, is history.

I became a Mennonite camp follower. Now the image of "camp follower" may not be appropriate for anyone pretending to have learned much from the Mennonites, since "camp follower" suggests both a military encampment as well as a lady who makes her living in a manner offensive not only to Mennonites but also to most Christians. However, like a camp follower I do not have an ecclesial home, so I whore after what I think is faithful to the gospel. I cannot pretend that such a position can be made ecclesially intelligible. My only defense is that God in our time seems to have led many of us to that point.[7] We live in a time when the theological battles of the past that seemed so important and justified Christian divisions simply no longer matter. (Consider, for example, the issue of being a "free will baptist.") That God has made some ecclesially homeless we can only pray will be the beginning of a unity, as John would put it, from the bottom up.[8] Yet the problem of the military imagery remains.

How Being a Pacifist Made Me a Warrior

I had become convinced that Yoder was doing work toward which I could not help but be sympathetic, given my own theological convictions. But I was not yet ready to declare myself a pacifist.[9] I remember clearly the first time I said I was a pacifist—a year later, I think. Robert Wilken had joined the Notre Dame faculty and I had begun to press David Burrell, the new chair of the department, to hire Yoder full time. Wilken, then a deeply committed Lutheran and, even worse, a graduate of the University of Chicago, was giving me a ride to faculty meeting and asking me about Yoder. He had great respect for what he had read of Yoder's work, but observed that he was unconvinced by Yoder's ecclesiology, in particular, his pacifism. For some reason I blurted out that Wilken was wrong and then I said it: "I am a pacifist."

Yoder had convinced me that you could not separate Christology and the question of nonviolence. So if I was to be fully Chalcedonian in my Christology, if I was to be fully Trinitarian in my doctrine of God, if I was to trust in God's providential care of creation through the calling of the church, then I had to be a pacifist. I have never regretted having so declared myself even though it has never felt like a decision "I made." Rather I am a pacifist because, given the way Yoder had taught me to think, I could not be anything else.

However, being a pacifist creates an entirely different way of thinking about theology. Of course, it is not just pacifism that does so, but rather the way Yoder teaches us to think about theology as a practice of the church. Indeed, it is a mistake to make pacifism *the* practice that isolates Christians from the many other practices necessary for the life of the church. For example, the obligation of Christians to tell one another the truth, to not lie, requires us to develop skillful modes of speech in order to say no more than needs to be said. I would not pretend that I learned all this from Yoder, but what I learned from Yoder has helped me see connections I otherwise might have missed.

As I began to write about Yoder—and in a manner that I had learned from him, at least to some extent—I began to be claimed by and to learn more about the world that had created John. I was invited several times to speak at the Associated Mennonite Biblical Seminary, where in 1978 I was given a copy of *Martyrs Mirror* in lieu of an honorarium. Well, that is not quite right. They said I could be paid twenty-five dollars or be given a copy of *Martyrs Mirror*. I was not stupid so I took the book, which had a lovely inscription naming me an "honorary Mennonite." Students from AMBS began to come to Notre Dame and take my courses. In the process I learned from these student, from what I was reading, as well as from John, that neither he or his work was universally accepted by other Mennonites. In other words, I quickly learned to distinguish Mennonite reality from Mennonite theology—but then that is a distinction that any good Mennonite makes. After all, it was from John that I learned to think of Mennonite farm culture as a form of Constantianism.

Yet I also had learned to see, in Mennonite life, habits that I might not have learned to see if my seeing had not been trained by John's work. For example, I learned to see how the lack of money can became a resource that enriches a community as it makes cooperation and agreements necessary for survival. Money or wealth can impoverish by robbing us of our need for one another and of the goods we hold in common—goods as basic as shared tractors. From this perspective, the liberal presumption that a community must find a way to balance the needs of the individual with the needs of the whole community makes no sense once the practices of the community are seen as being more primary than whatever we mean by individual or community. John also taught me to see in Mennonite life that theology had to be understood as just one more practice of a people who have learned that their lives depend on learning how to share their lives.

John probably thought I continued to read more philosophy than was good for me, but then I was not fortunate to have had the philosophical foundation that he had, nor did I—or do I—possess his extraordinary intelligence. He could never understand my difficulty in learning other languages. I needed to read more in order to learn how to do theology in the apparently effortless manner that I saw in John.

If my "thought" or "scholarship" reflects my encounter with Anabaptist thought, that direction is more clearly exhibited in the "how" than in the "what" of my work. In particular, I do not think that theology is "thought" that can be abstracted from the practices of a people. In the current academic world this understanding of theology is obviously problematic. I have tried to develop the polemics needed to gain Yoder a hearing in the university as well as the wider church. John, I suspect, thought I was and am far too "contrary"—but then he did not come, as I did, from the mainstream. If "my work" is understood as but a footnote to Yoder, I will think God has used me well indeed.

John, however, would probably worry about how Mennonites might be influenced by me, since my theological work does not appropriately attend to the actual text of the scripture in the manner that John so wonderfully exemplified in his work. For example, I would love to be able to write a book like *He Came Preaching Peace*, but I simply do not have

John's extraordinary knowledge of the Scriptures or his uncanny ability to see the connection between texts.[10] Some readers tell me that my work is "biblical," but being "biblical" is not enough.[11] The text and the words matter, and Yoder knew how to make them matter. I hope someone may soon try to show how Yoder did not simply "use" scripture, but rather how he reasoned scripturally.[12]

That is no small matter. I currently have three Mennonite graduate students: Chris Huebner, Alex Sider, and Peter Dula. They represent different streams in Mennonite life but they are all "well formed" Mennonites. I want the training they receive at Duke to serve the upbuilding of the church. I do not want to hurt them, but all I can do is teach them what I have been taught. Of course they read Yoder, but do Mennonites really need to know much about Aristotle, Aquinas, MacIntyre, and Milbank in order to do theology in the Anabaptist tradition? Will they pick up bad habits—at least bad habits for Mennonites—from me? I hope not, but all I can do is hope. At the very least I hope that as they are "reintegrated" into the Mennonite world, what they have learned will help all of us know better how to survive as people committed to Christian nonviolence and how that commitment shapes the way theology should be done.

What Bugs Me About Mennonites

It would be pretentious for me to pontificate about what I do not like about Mennonite theology or Mennonite life, since I obviously do not know that much about either. What I know is Yoder, but I do not know what Yoder knew. Of course, I have read books here and essays there by and about Mennonites, but I certainly do not know Mennonite sources or developments in Mennonite theology over the centuries. Having three Mennonite graduate students is helpful, however, because they make me read what I otherwise would not even know existed. For example, Sider and Dula recently asked me to read Marpeck's "Judgment and Decision." I was struck by how similar Marpeck is to Yoder, which, of course, gets it backwards. But then that is how I learned it—backwards.

For example, Marpeck comments on who should be avoided:

> But I will have nothing to do with any other sect, faction, or gathering, no matter what they are called in the whole world. I will especially avoid those who use bodily sword, contrary to the patience of Christ, who did not resist any evil and who likewise commands His own not to resist tribulation or evil, in order to rule in the kingdom of Christ. I also avoid those who institute, command, and forbid, therewith to lead and rule the kingdom of Christ. I also avoid those who deny the true divinity, Spirit, Word, and power in Jesus Christ. I avoid those who destroy and deny His natural, earthly humanity which was received from man, of the seed of David, born without man's seed and sin, born of Mary the pure virgin; He was crucified and died a natural earthly death, from which He arose again, and has now seated Himself at the right hand of God. I also avoid those who, living in open sin and gross evil, want to have fellowship in the kingdom of Christ but without true repentance, and I avoid all those who tolerate such a thing. I avoid all who oppose and fight against the words and the truth of Christ. With all such regardless of what they are called in the world, I will have no part or fellowship in the kingdom of Christ unless they repent.[13]

This may seem to be an unremarkable passage, but what I find so interesting is Marpeck's list, as well as how it is ordered. The use of the "bodily sword" and the confession that Jesus was fully God and fully man are all part of what makes the body of Christ the body of Christ. Indeed the disavowal of the sword and the confession that Christ is who he said he was are not separable. As I suggested above, I learned from Yoder that the practice of nonviolence must be shaped by Christological convictions. But the items on Marpeck's list are connected in another way that is equally important in terms of the crucial challenges before Mennonite life: Marpeck and Yoder both assume that in spite of Anabaptist dissent, Anabaptists remain in continuity with the church catholic and, in particular, with Christological developments. Yet this presumption as well and its implications are denied by many Anabaptists.

That continuity with Catholic Christianity is often denied by Anabaptists is quite understandable. You seldom find yourself in continuity with those who kill you. Moreover, the very fact that Anabaptists were forced to become "Anabaptist" could not help but underwrite the assumption that Mennonites have to "reinvent" Christianity.[14] Yet the idea that somehow the Mennonites are "starting over" is not only theologically doubtful but particularly dangerous in modernity. Theologically it is simply a mistake to assume that God has ever left the world without a faithful witness. The fact that the church is often a witness against itself is but a testimony to God's care of God's church and world. The crucial issue, of course, is what ecclesiological form is best equipped to tell the story of God's faithful care of the church.

Even though I think Denny Weaver is wrong to argue that the ecumenical creeds are compromised by the Constantinian character of the church that produced them, we are in his debt for raising the issue so forcefully. Indeed I believe the recent discussion initiated by Gerald Schlabach and Ivan Kaufmann between Mennonites and Catholics is an extraordinarily important development. We now have a forum where these questions can be investigated with the kind of thoroughness they deserve. What makes this development so promising is that it is not a matter of Mennonites *opposing* Catholics, since we have Catholics (such as Mike Baxter) who, without being any less Catholic, represent Anabaptist commitments, and we have Anabaptists (like Schlabach) who, without being less Anabaptist, have deep Catholic sensibilities.[15]

Moreover, it would be a mistake to think that the question of the relation between Mennonites and Catholics is primarily about "doctrine," even the doctrine of the church. As I tried to argue in "Whose Church? Which Future? Whither the Anabaptist Vision?" the challenge facing Anabaptists is to discover the implications of living in a world in which they have won.[16] Constantinianism has been defeated. There is no established church for Anabaptists to oppose. Christianity has become voluntary, but the voluntary-ness constituted by modernity makes it impossible to maintain the disciplines necessary to be nonviolent. As is often the case, the terms of the battles of the past may not prepare us well for the challenges we now face.

To suggest that Mennonites need to reconsider their relation with Catholics may only confirm the presumption of many that my unhappy state as a Methodist tempts me to romanticize Mennonites and Catholics. I cannot pretend to be free of that temptation, but Catholic and Mennonite reality is always a welcome check on any form of such romanticization.[17] There is much more at stake in the Mennonite/ Catholic interaction than mutual sharing of the other's "insights." The unity of Christ's body I take to be the crucial issue—the "issue" that is also at the heart of what it means to be nonviolent.

However, the word "Catholic" does name a reality that Mennonites desperately need. If I were forced to name any aspect of Mennonite life that I find problematic, it would be how Mennonites worship. Mennonite hymnody is obviously a great resource, but I have found Mennonite liturgy generally to be rationalistic and aesthetically thin. Zwingli's rationalistic tendencies have won. For example, believer's baptism invites presumptions that the baptized must "know what they are doing," which in modernity makes the agent of this act the one being baptized rather than God. My problem with believer's baptism has always been what it does for those we unhappily call the "mentally handicapped." If the issue, as Yoder argues, is the question of the baptized being accountable to the church, I do not see why the profoundly mentally handicapped cannot be baptized and held accountable in using their gifts on behalf of the church. The body into which we are baptized is not the individualized body we think of as "ours," but rather Christ's body.[18]

That same body is what we also receive in the Eucharist. When I taught at Notre Dame I often had Catholics who admired the witness of Mennonites say they did not know how Mennonites sustained their nonviolence with infrequent eucharistic celebration. I tried to defend Mennonite practice by pointing out that Mennonites use eucharistic language, but that language "fits" over the way they think their lives must be lived. I continue to regard that as a legitimate response. But I also think that the Mennonite practice—or the absence of the practice—threatens to makes Mennonites' lives unintelligible. The Eucharist is not the sacrifice we make to an eternally angry God to try to buy ourselves some time; rather, the Eucharist is the good news that God would have us included in Christ's sacrifice for the world so that the world may have an alternative to pointless and endless sacrifice.

The celebration of the Eucharist, moreover, cannot be separated from questions regarding the shape of the liturgy as well as who is to preside at the celebration of the Eucharist. Questions of ordination and authority cannot be kept at bay if Mennonites are to undertake any reform of worship, which I hope they will indeed do. The alternatives seem to be ethnic identity or church growth strategies. The former has been tried and found wanting; the latter is too ugly to contemplate. But I want to be clear. I am not suggesting that Mennonites should try to mimic Catholic liturgy. Rather, Mennonites need to consider, in a manner faithful to Mennonite life, why Word and Table cannot be separated.

When I described myself as a "high church Mennonite" many years ago I was not kidding. I am, after all, a Methodist and heir to that unstable brew that is, at least if we take Wesley seriously, at once evangelical and Catholic. Methodists are, or at least should be, free church sacramentalists as well as sanctificationists. Only God knows whether that finally amounts to a coherent ecclesiology, but it at least helps explain why it makes me so happy that some

Mennonites find some of what I do useful. I can only pray that we—Catholics, Methodists, Mennonites—will arrive at the moment when we can only make sense of what God has done with us by sharing our stories.

CHAPTER THREE

Following Christ Down Under: A New Zealand Perspective on Anabaptism

Christopher Marshall

To say we were converted by a cookbook would be going too far. But it was the *More with Less* recipe book, together with John Howard Yoder's *The Politics of Jesus*, which my wife Margaret and I read as university students, that first triggered our interest in the Anabaptist tradition. Both books were produced by Mennonites and both gave expression, in different ways, to the same fundamental Anabaptist conviction: that to be a Christian means following Jesus; that following Jesus means taking Jesus' ethical teaching seriously; and that taking Jesus seriously means a lifestyle of simplicity, service, and peacemaking. In the heyday of student radicalism in the early 1970s, discovering the authentic Christian radicalism of this long-established faith tradition—little known in New Zealand—was very timely. Three decades later we regard that tradition as one of the most formative influences on our understanding of Christian faith. Our lives have been immeasurably enriched by participation in two Mennonite congregations, attendance at several Mennonite conferences, periods of sabbatical leave at Mennonite seminaries and, above all, by enduring friendships with Mennonite Christians in different parts of the world.

First Contact

After completing my initial theological studies in New Zealand in 1980, I was accepted for doctoral work in New Testament at the University of London. We decided to spend three months in North America en route to Britain. Thinking that this visit would be a good opportunity to meet some real live Mennonites, I obtained addresses of three Mennonite organizations from the U.S. embassy in New Zealand. One was near Chicago, which was on our itinerary, so we arranged to pay them a visit.

Our first few weeks in America were unsettling. We encountered various expressions of church life, but disliked much of what we saw. Whether it was the smooth consumer religion of the mega-church we visited in Los Angeles, or the manipulative showmanship of the countless televangelists we masochistically watched, or the overt racism of the small midwestern Presbyterian church we attended with some distant relations, the American Christian scene seemed bizarre indeed. Most disturbing, however, was the boisterous "God and country" nationalism that seemed to permeate church as well as society. I remember watching one well known TV preacher—whose theology was "thoroughly orthodox," I was assured by an American friend—commemorate the Fourth of July with a sermon entitled, "I am the American flag." In return for a reasonable donation to his ministry, I could have received a transcript of his message and a lapel badge of the Stars and Stripes. I resisted the temptation.

With all this fresh in our minds, we turned up at the Mennonite World Conference headquarters in Lombard, near Chicago, where we were given a gracious welcome and spent the afternoon in conversation. At one point I asked the director, the late Paul Kraybill, what he thought of the religious nationalism so pervasive in what we had seen of the American church. "Idolatry!" was his simple reply. I recall writing in the visitors book: "Wonderful to meet kindred spirits."

We arrived in England later that year and spent the first

few months settling in. We visited several churches in our neighborhood but could find nothing that really suited us. One weekend I went with a friend to a conference celebrating the fifth birthday of the British magazine *Third Way*. One of the speakers was Alan Kreider, director of the London Mennonite Centre. I was most impressed with him, and the following Sunday we attended the worship service of the London Mennonite Fellowship in Highgate, North London. To us as strangers in a foreign land, it felt like coming home spiritually. We fitted, in a way we had not experienced before. We remained active members of that church until we returned to New Zealand four years later.

What did we find so special in this small Mennonite fellowship? Many things. But the one that stands out was its holistic, integrative approach to Christian life. Here was a church that attempted to hold together many of the concerns we had come to believe were integral to Christian faith but that Christians so often set against each other: joyful worship with sensitivity to the world's pain; thoughtful biblical teaching with openness to the Spirit; evangelistic concern with social commitment; scholarship with spirituality; ethical seriousness with humility and gentleness; Christian community with an acceptance of people's individuality; enjoyment of cultural activities with nonconformity to the world. These concerns often appear to be mutually exclusive in Christian circles—we split asunder what God has joined together. Yet, the London Mennonite community, at this early and vibrant stage of its development, aspired to a natural and attractive integration of them.

During the four years of our membership in this church I first acquired an appreciation for the distinctive features of Anabaptist theology and practice. It came less from reading Anabaptist literature (though I did some of that too) and more from valued friendships and dialogue. Two other factors heightened my incentive to learn about Anabaptism. One was the area of my doctoral research. When initially contemplating dissertation topics in New Zealand, I had made a conscious decision to work in the gospels rather than the epistles. This was partly because I wanted the benefit of expert scholarly guidance on how to read the synoptic accounts, given their inherent source-critical complexity, but mainly because in my own Protestant background the gospel narratives were all but ignored outside the children's Sunday school room. I ended up writing a Ph.D. dissertation on the meaning and function of faith in the Gospel of Mark.[1] Working on the thesis brought me face to face with Jesus' radical call to discipleship, with all its subversive political and lifestyle implications.

The other factor that added urgency to my desire to understand Anabaptism was the outbreak of the Falklands/Malvinas war between Britain and Argentina in 1982. Coming from a small, peaceful nation at the bottom of the world, I experienced life for the first time in a country gearing up for war. And, as one would expect of a nation that excels in military pageantry, Britain did it with great efficiency. I remember being struck by the speed with which the mass media were commandeered for propaganda purposes. The pressure to fall in behind the nation's military commitment was almost overwhelming. Even as a visitor I was susceptible to it. Also memorable was the deafening silence of the mainstream churches as preparations for war began. Weeks passed before the Anglican church, the established church of the nation, spoke out publicly on the impending conflict, and only then to give its qualified support for the campaign.

So, in retrospect, I was a likely candidate for an Anabaptist conversion—a Ph.D. student working in the gospel traditions while attending a pacifist church in the capital city of a country suddenly at war. And it was precisely the congruence of central Anabaptist convictions with impinging political realities on the one hand, and major themes in the gospel story on the other, that led me to embrace Anabaptism. Not that I simply adopted a ready-made denominational or ideological package in toto. It was more a matter of discovery that a broadly Anabaptist approach to Christian faith squared satisfyingly with the New Testament records, as I was learning to read them, and with the needs and priorities of the post-Christendom world, which now confronts us. My overriding feeling was, "This is what I've been looking for."

In 1986 I returned to New Zealand to take up a lecturing post at an evangelical theological institution in Auckland, where I still teach today. This has been a very different context for continuing to develop an appreciation of Anabaptism, one in which the terms "Mennonite" and "Anabaptist" are known chiefly from Reformation history textbooks, since there are no Mennonite or self-declared Anabaptist churches in New Zealand. Within this setting I have found that claiming an Anabaptist-Mennonite identity has afforded me a distinctive position on the left wing of the New Zealand evangelical constituency. It has become, in the language of New Zealand's indigenous Maori people, my *turangawaewae*, my "place to stand." From this place, I am able to affirm what both traditions hold in common, as well as to offer a sympathetic critique of evangelical priorities and practices in light of Anabaptist insights. I am also able to engage in wider ecumenical conversations from a perspective that regards socio-political and evangelistic commitments as equally authentic expressions of gospel witness.

None of this is to say that I feel a special responsibility to promote Anabaptism per se. My primary calling is to teach the New Testament. Any Anabaptist perspectives I communicate to others usually come indirectly through my exposition of the biblical text rather than through deliberate proselytizing, which is no doubt how the early Anabaptists would have wanted it to be. It is also a peculiarly effective way to subvert evangelical defenses, since evangelicals have a self-perception—or self-deception—of being the only Christians to take biblical authority seriously. If I were to try to commend the Anabaptist vision on the authority of Mennonite authors, I would encounter polite uninterest. But when such a vision emerges as a result of grappling with the biblical text, students feel obligated to listen, and profound shifts in their thinking often result. Witnessing such changes gives me more vocational satisfaction than anything else I do.

Gains from Anabaptism

What other gains has Anabaptism offered me as a theological educator? Chief among them is what could be called its integrative Christocentrism. From Anabaptism I have learned that the essential mark of Christian identity is not simply a correct theological evaluation of the person and work of Christ but a conformity to the way of life taught and demonstrated by Jesus in the gospel records. From this has come the capacity to integrate the diverse interests I mentioned earlier: joyful worship with sensitivity to pain; disciplined teaching with openness to the Spirit; and an equal concern for scholarship and spirituality, for community and individuality, for cultural engagement and nonconformity to the world, for evangelism and social action. I am not suggesting that such integration is typical of most Anabaptist or Mennonite communities, either historically or currently. Sadly not. Like all Christian traditions and denominations, there is diversity, as well as compromise, failure, and atrophy within the Anabaptist fold, just as there are many Christian communities outside the Anabaptist tradition that are healthier examples of integration than those within. What I am suggesting is that it is Anabaptism's central commitment to the paradigmatic significance of Jesus' life and teaching that offers the soundest basis for genuine integration to occur. In his own life and ministry Jesus embodied the holistic embrace of God's kingdom. He addressed with equal concern the spiritual, physical, and social dimensions of life.[2] If Jesus displayed an inclusive wholesomeness of life, then those who look to the story of Jesus for their model of Christian conduct should surely strive to do so as well.

Of course, all Christian traditions are Christocentric, which is what makes them "Christian" in the first place. But in the mainstream traditions, doctrinal Christocentrism has tended to eclipse ethical Christocentrism. In other words, what one believes about Christ has been more important than whether one actually obeys him in action. Christ has functioned more as the central link in the doctrine of salvation than as the primary source of Christian values and praxis. Tellingly, the church's historic creeds are all but silent on ethics in general and the strenuous demands of Jesus in particular. That has allowed the church historically to bear the name of Christ but to do the work of the devil at the same time. In the interests of doctrinal orthodoxy, the church has raised armies and waged war, tortured heretics and burned witches, persecuted dissenters and compelled conversions. In a way, the Anabaptist-Mennonite tradition emerged as, and in certain crucial respects remains, a protest movement against the moral compromises and cultural captivity of mainstream Christianity.

The ethical Christocentrism of Anabaptism has also furnished me with a hermeneutical framework for thinking about how the scriptures are to be applied today. The framework rests on three principal convictions. The first is that the proper setting for scriptural interpretation is the gathered community of believers, under the guidance of the Holy Spirit. Hermeneutics is essentially a communal affair; it is not the special preserve of theological scholars or the ecclesiastical hierarchy, but belongs to the whole people of God operating as a pneumatic democracy.[3] Since the task of the Spirit in the discernment process is to bring to the community's remembrance what the earthly Jesus taught (Jn. 14:26), a second key conviction follows: Whatever in scripture agrees with Jesus' teaching and example conveys God's word for today; whatever contradicts the way of Jesus, such as war, racial separation or capital punishment, is no longer God's intention for the new covenant community. Accordingly, as Richard Hays puts it, "If irreconcilable tensions exist between the moral vision of the New Testament and that of particular Old Testament texts, the New Testament vision trumps the Old Testament."[4]

These two convictions depend on the third: In order to understand truly what is written about Christ in scripture and what is consistent with his teaching and spirit, one must also walk with Christ on the path of costly obedience. Hans Denck put this point memorably: "No one can claim truly to know Christ unless one follows him in life." Jürgen Moltmann glosses this saying aptly: "There is no Christology without Christopraxis, no knowledge of Christ without the practice of Christ. We cannot grasp Christ merely with our heads or our hearts. We come to understand him through a total, all-embracing practice of living; and that means discipleship."[5] Moltmann's citation of Denck illustrates how this key Anabaptist hermeneutical axiom, that we can only know the truth insofar as we live the truth, has come to the fore in much recent biblical and theological scholarship. It is also peculiarly suited to the postmodern context in which we now live, with its emphasis on experiential truth and "walking the talk."

So the integrative Christocentrism of Anabaptism—its emphasis on the centrality of Jesus for ethics and hermeneutics as well as for salvation and theology—has significantly shaped my appreciation of the theological task.

So has the Anabaptist commitment to peace theology. Mennonite colleagues have taught me that it is not only possible to "do" theology from a self-consciously pacifist stance, but that, when one does so, fresh insights and emphases emerge. I have found this to be true in my own work. I have just completed a book that attempts to furnish biblical and theological foundations for the so-called restorative justice movement within current criminological practice.[6] Its central thesis is that the biblical witness to God's justice is better characterized in restorative or redemptive categories than in retributive or punitive ones. Two of the biggest hurdles I faced in arguing for this thesis are New Testament passages about final judgment that anticipate wrath and damnation on God's enemies, and popular theologies of the atonement that attribute the salvific power of the cross to some cosmic act of substitutionary punishment. In both cases, God's justice appears to be definitively vindicated through violent, death-dealing retribution, something that has disturbing implications for peace theology and practice.

Now it is true that Christian nonviolence does not strictly depend on the supposition of a nonviolent God.[7] But it makes much better sense theologically to believe that Jesus practiced nonviolence and demanded it of his followers, because nonviolence corresponds to the essential nature of the deity (Mt. 5:9, 43-48), of whom Christ is the visible image (Col. 1:15; Heb. 1:1-4). This conviction forced me to go behind the violent imagery so often used in the New Testament for eschatological judgment, not least by Jesus himself, to seek a non-retributive or nonviolent way of understanding the doctrine of hell, yet one that remains faithful to the somber warnings of scripture about the possibility of final separation. The same is true with penal conceptions of the atonement. In wrestling with the work of the cross from a pacifist perspective, I have come to believe that the power of sin was broken, not by some act of substitutionary punishment but through Jesus' own definitive refusal to perpetuate the cycle of violence and revenge. In his passion, Jesus adopted the position of supreme victim of human evil and depredation. Yet he refused to respond to his victimization by victimizing those who victimized him. Instead he absorbed human violence without retaliation. "When he was abused, he did not return abuse; when he suffered, he did not threaten; but he entrusted himself to the one who judges justly. He himself *bore our sins in his body on the cross*, so that free from sins, we might live for righteousness . . ." (1 Pet. 2:23-24, emphasis mine). In so doing Jesus broke the mimetic or pay-back mechanism that lies at the heart of sin's power and unleashed the liberative power of forgiveness (Lk. 23:34). This dimension of the cross is largely ignored in standard theologies of atonement, but it emerges powerfully when the "mystery of salvation" is viewed in light of a theologically grounded Anabaptist pacifism.

Some Limitations

While happily claiming an Anabaptist-Mennonite identity in the Christian setting in which I work, I do not believe that Anabaptism has all the answers. Nor has Anabaptism been the only formative influence on my understanding of Christian discipleship. Charismatic and contemplative spiritualities have also played a part, as have certain features of the Reformed tradition, though more at a philosophical than a theological or experiential level. As a university student, I was part of a study group that drank deeply from the wells of Herman Dooyeweerd's Reformational philosophy. I don't pretend to have understood all, or even most, of what I read or heard in those days. But I grasped enough to become convinced that Christian faith must be applied to all areas of human life and learning, not just to religious and moral areas, for if Christ is not Lord of all, he is not Lord at all. This theocratic ideal in Reformed thinking has provided a helpful corrective to the unhealthy separatism that has plagued the Anabaptist tradition.

I proposed earlier that Anabaptist Christocentrism provides the firmest foundation for an integrative or holistic theology, but that historically this potential has not been much realized in the Anabaptist movement itself. The "two kingdoms" theology of Schleitheim, born of intense persecution, has often solidified into a thoroughgoing dualism that effectively abandons the world in favor of the Christian ghetto, even in more benign environments than sixteenth-century Europe. The legacy of this sectarian tendency has been that neither Anabaptist piety nor Anabaptist scholarship has given much detailed thought to how the Christian worldview should shape our understanding of all areas of human endeavor, including those "outside the perfection of Christ." It may be true, as Anabaptist critics have urged, that in their attempt to provide a workable program for Caesar, mainstream Christian traditions have compromised the ethical distinctives of Christian discipleship. But that does not invalidate the importance, and missional imperative, of seeking to conform the whole of human life—individual and social, ecclesial and worldly—to Christ's lordship. In my experience, Anabaptist scholarship on such matters is yet to approach the sophistication and profundity of Christian learning that I have encountered in neo-Reformed circles.[8]

Recently I visited the Institute for Christian Studies in Toronto, a Christian graduate school devoted to theoretical reflection on the meaning and integrity of all major areas of created reality from a self-consciously Reformational perspective. Toward the end of a fascinating discussion with four faculty members, one commented that the Reformed tradition needed Anabaptism to keep it honest. "We are easily seduced by power," he said. The Anabaptist emphasis on the way of the cross offered an important antidote, he suggested, to the Reformed temptation to achieve valid goals by coercive means. I replied that Anabaptism also needs the Reformed tradition—to keep it from the ghetto, to keep its concern for nonconformity to the world from degenerating into non-commitment to the world, and to preclude pacifism becoming passivism in face of injustice.

Until recently, justice has not figured as prominently on the Anabaptist agenda as peace, and peace has been traditionally understood in terms of nonresistance. But peace is a complex virtue. It involves more than eschewing lethal violence, for violence is systemically embedded in human social structures and cannot be entirely avoided by anyone. Indeed sometimes the very attempt to escape being personally implicated in overt violence may serve further to entrench and nurture hidden, systemic violence. It is the embeddedness, subtlety, and tenacity of violence that makes justice such an indispensable ingredient in genuine peacemaking, lest peacemaking be coopted by evil powers as a means of preserving unjust and violent structures. This truth has forced itself on Anabaptist thinkers as the rural isolation and sectarian separatism of the past have given way to a more socially engaged stance. Again at this juncture Anabaptism has much to learn from the experience of other Christian traditions that have long wrestled with the ambiguities and compromises of working out justice in an unjust world.

This presupposes that Anabaptists should dialogue with and welcome the wisdom of other Christian traditions. I have sometimes sensed a tension at this point in North American Mennonite circles. It is a tension between the peacemaker's desire to embrace others and the minority movement's fear of losing or diluting its distinctive ethnic and cultural identity. As an outsider, I have found this Mennonite consciousness of possessing a special identity both attractive and daunting. Its appeal has been the sense of solidarity and continuity with the past that it generates. Its drawback has been the barrier to belonging that it creates, the feeling that unless one is born of Mennonite stock one is not truly a Mennonite. This is unintentional, and all the Mennonites I know would in principle firmly resist any thought of ethnicity serving as a surrogate badge of membership, since voluntary submission to Christ is the heart of the Anabaptist ideal. But in practice it is a challenge for a minority group simultaneously to treasure its historical sense of peoplehood and unreservedly embrace those people who are drawn to the fruits but lack the roots.

I am enormously grateful for my exposure to Anabaptist theology and practice. It continues to nourish my Christian faith and to inform my Christian thinking. I remain convinced that as Christendom unravels before our eyes and the Western church is forced by this fact to rethink its true role in society, Anabaptism is an idea that has found its day. But it is not an idea that is autonomous and all-conquering. Anabaptism has many strengths, but it also has blind spots and limitations. Perhaps the future belongs to so-called "hyphenated Anabaptists," believers who espouse the essence of the Anabaptist vision but who seek to marry it with the insights and wisdom of their own traditions. Such hyphenated Anabaptists, like the teachers of the law in Jesus' saying who have been trained in the kingdom of heaven, are "like the master of a household who brings out of his treasure what is new and what is old" (Mt. 13:52).

CHAPTER FOUR

Anabaptist Science and Epistemology?

Nancey Murphy

I first encountered Anabaptist theology at the Graduate Theological Union in Berkeley where I had gone to pursue a doctorate in theology, with James William McClendon Jr. as my advisor. His first advice to me was, "I strongly recommend that you take my seminar," a course on Radical Reformation history and theology.

That was the second time my academic life had been changed by an advisor "encouraging" me to take a course I otherwise would have avoided. On the first occasion I was majoring in psychology at Creighton University and my advisor there urged me to take a course in philosophy of science. The course was so exciting that I chose to pursue a doctorate in that field. Near the end of that program, at the University of California, Berkeley, I again decided to change fields, one reason being that I judged I did not know enough about science itself to make a significant contribution to the philosophy of science. Meanwhile I had encountered intellectual atheism for the first time, after thirteen years in Catholic parochial schools and a degree from a Jesuit university, and realized that the problems associated with the rationality of Christian belief were more challenging and personally engaging than were problems in the philosophy of science. But if one needed to know science—especially, in those days, physics—to be a competent philosopher of science, surely one needed to know theology in order to be a competent philosopher of religion. Hence my decision to take a second doctorate at the neighboring GTU—and my encounter with McClendon.

The theology I encountered in McClendon's seminar was attractive. I was drawn to a theology that incorporated congregational church polity because, in my years of participation in a Catholic charismatic prayer group, I had come to see that biblical talk of "church" applied more readily to a small congregation, such as our prayer group, than it did to an international institution. And, in general, the Anabaptist understanding of what Christianity is basically all about— articulated best by John Howard Yoder—seemed to fit the New Testament better than many other versions of Christian thought and practice. However, it was reading about the widespread torture and killing of Anabaptists, especially the martyrdom of Michael Sattler, that had the greatest immediate impact on my life. Clearly, if Jesus had to choose between the ones being killed and the ones doing the killing, both Catholic and Protestant, he would be on the side of the ones who were dying. I felt a claim on my life at that time—to join a church in which refraining from killing fellow Christians was not an optional extra. I had become a "just-war pacifist" at Creighton University during the Vietnam era. The Catholic church provided criteria for a just war, including proportionality, and I judged that no war, especially in our age, could meet those requirements. So I saw pacifism as consistent with Catholic teaching but, of course, not obligatory for Catholics. It was only when I moved to Pasadena eight years later that I—with, by then, my husband James McClendon—was able to join a church explicitly Anabaptist in its self-understanding (Pasadena Church of the Brethren).

In the meantime my academic interests had taken another turn due to the influence of Robert J. Russell, a physicist and theologian, who founded the Center for Theology and the Natural Sciences at the GTU the year after I arrived there. Russell invited me to contribute my expertise in philosophy of science and philosophy of religion to various projects sponsored by the Center. Growing public as well as scholarly interest in the relations between theology and science meant increasingly frequent invitations to attend conferences and to lecture in that area. The most exciting project has been a series of conferences, sponsored by CTNS and the Vatican Observatory, examining the consequences of various scientific advances for a Christian understanding of God's action in the natural world. The first conference considered two scientific issues: "quantum cosmology" (Stephen Hawking's idea that time would have had no directionality in the early universe and hence the universe could have had no "beginning"); and the "fine-tuning" of the laws of nature (recognition of the a priori improbability of having a universe in which all constants and laws fit within the narrow boundaries required for a universe that would permit life).[1]

At that conference I met George F. R. Ellis, a mathematician and cosmologist from the University of Cape Town, and also a Quaker deeply involved in the anti-apartheid struggle. It happened that we both had an extra day to spend in Castel Gandolfo, site of the Vatican Observatory, and while walking around lovely Lake Albano we asked ourselves whether the abstruse physics we had been considering for the past week had anything to do with real life. For Ellis, "real life" was the dangerous situation in South Africa; for me it was the buildup to the Gulf War. Neither of us had an answer. In addition, both of us were dissatisfied with the mainline theology that seemed always to be assumed without question in theology and science dialogues.

Several months later Ellis sent me an outline for a book he wanted us to write together. This was a chance to investigate whether the science-theology dialogue and Anabaptist theology had anything to say to one another. The result was our co-authored volume, *On the Moral Nature of the Universe: Theology, Cosmology, and Ethics*.[2] Here is how we summarized our position in the preface:

The (apparent) fine-tuning of the cosmological constants to produce a life-bearing universe (the anthropic issue) seems to call for explanation. A theistic explanation allows for a more coherent account of reality—as we know it from the perspective of both natural and human sciences, and from other spheres of experience such as the moral sphere—than does a non-theistic account. However, not all accounts of the divine nature are consistent with the patterns of divine action we seem to perceive in the natural world. God appears to work in concert with nature, never overriding or violating the very processes that God has created. This account of the character of divine action as refusal to do violence to creation, whatever the cost to God, has direct implications for human morality; it implies a "kenotic" or self-renunciatory ethic, according to which one must renounce self-interest for the sake of the other, no matter what the cost to oneself. Such an ethic, however, is very much at variance with ethical presuppositions embedded in current social science. Hence, new research programs are called for in these fields, exploring the possibilities for human sociality in the light of a vision modeled on God's own self-sacrificing love. . . .

Much of the book is a synthesis and development of the work of others. We employ the philosophy of science and epistemology of Carl Hempel, Imre Lakatos, and Alasdair MacIntyre to understand the forms of reasoning that we need in order to justify our claims. Arthur Peacocke has developed a model for relating theology and the sciences that employs the idea of a "hierarchy of sciences"; he suggests that theology be understood as the science at the top of the hierarchy. What is new in our synthesis is, first, the proposal that the hierarchy be split at the higher levels into natural- and human-science branches, and, second, that the human-science branch should have at its top the "science" of ethics. It is then possible to see theology as the discipline that completes both branches—answering "boundary questions," which arise in both cosmology and ethics, yet going beyond the scope of those disciplines alone. A single account of the divine purposes in creation, then, drawn largely from the work of John Howard Yoder, provides a bridge between the natural sciences and the human sciences.

I was given another opportunity to pursue relations between Anabaptist theology and science when McClendon asked me to write a chapter on science for the third volume of his systematic theology, *Witness*, a volume on theology and culture written from the perspective of the Radical Reformation.[3] Here I argue that there has been a complex interaction among Darwinian theory, Christianity, and social ethics. While it is well known that ethical views have been (and continue to be) derived from evolutionary biology, what is not always appreciated is the extent to which Darwin's account of natural processes was a product of the economic, ethical, and natural-theological theories of his own day. My claim, further, is that the Anabaptist concept of "the gospel of all creatures"[4] calls into question alliances between evolutionary theory and social policy that are based on the dominance of conflictual images such as "the struggle for existence" and "the survival of the fittest." On that basis I question the negative images of both nature and God that Darwinism has been taken to sponsor. And, as it turns out, biologists themselves have moved toward a more "pacifist" account of the natural world.[5]

I find it ironic that, having left the philosophy of science and gone into the philosophy of religion to avoid always being in a position where I was talking about science without detailed knowledge of the content of science, I have ended up spending a large part of my life since then talking about science!

What I meant to do instead was to study theology from the point of view of philosophy—from what I often call an Anglo-American postmodern perspective. However, since the qualifier is often overlooked, I am often classed with Continental postmodern thinkers, and so might more safely describe my philosophical stance as post-analytic. The philosophers who provide rich resources for me in rethinking questions in philosophical theology include Ludwig

Wittgenstein, W. V. O. Quine, J. L. Austin, and Imre Lakatos. Most useful (although he would distance himself further from analytic philosophy than these others do) is Alasdair MacIntyre. I have argued that MacIntyre's account of relations among the concepts of virtue, narrative, practice, and tradition is very helpful for understanding moves made by narrative and Anabaptist ethicists such as McClendon, Yoder, and Stanley Hauerwas. I am still puzzling over the question of whether it is more than historical accident that narrative ethics has come to be so closely associated with a Radical Reformation perspective on church.[6]

I have also argued that MacIntyre provides the best available resources for addressing the question central to the whole of my academic pursuits: the rationality of Christian belief. MacIntyre's argument for the tradition-dependence of all reasoning means that Christians need not apologize for the particularity of their historical starting point. All traditions, not just the Christian tradition, depend on authoritative texts. In addition, MacIntyre provides detailed historical examples and arguments to show that a plurality of traditions need not imply relativism: arguments, in the public domain, for a particular tradition's rational superiority to its rivals are in fact sometimes possible.[7]

The intriguing question regarding MacIntyre's contributions to epistemology arises from the fact that he is consciously working within the Thomist tradition and sees his own epistemological insights as "theology-laden" (my term). So I and my Mennonite doctoral student[8] have been discussing whether there is anything about MacIntyre's understanding of rationality of which a good Anabaptist should be suspicious. I began formulating an answer to this question in a lecture on Mennonite higher education at Canadian Mennonite Bible College in June of 1997. More recently I received an invitation to contribute to a book on epistemology from the perspectives of various Christian sub-traditions.[9] There I argue that an appropriately Anabaptist understanding of reason can be developed from MacIntyre's work by tempering his overly optimistic view of social practices with a Yoderian account of the principalities and powers.

My work on "Anabaptist epistemology" leads me to raise a question about the very ambiguity of an "Anabaptist approach to theology." The most standard approach would refer to the content of Anabaptist theology (as opposed to, say, Reformed or Catholic theology) and perhaps to general tendencies such as the privileging of ethics and practice over doctrine. But I have been asking how academic practice would change if we attempted to emulate as much as possible the shape of Anabaptist practices of communal judgment. Is there an Anabaptist approach to theology in this sense? Is there an appropriately communal way of doing theology, in the midst of our highly individualistic academic culture? I reflected briefly on this issue in a lecture at Eastern Mennonite University in March of 2000, "Traditions, Practices, and the Powers."

My current research focuses on neuroscience and philosophy of mind. I argue for a physicalist (as opposed to dualist or trichotomist) account of human nature on the grounds that it is the brain that accounts for all the human capacities once attributed to the soul. Improbable though it may seem, there are connections here, too, with Anabaptist theology. Despite the fact that biblical scholars and historians of doctrine have, for a century now, been disputing the dualism popularly attributed to the Scriptures, some Christian scholars remain committed to dualism because it is apparently the only way to account for the "intermediate state," a period of conscious awareness of God after death and prior to the general resurrection. However, Anabaptist writers never made this a part of their teaching, and many argued instead for "soul sleep," which could mean either the unconsciousness of a surviving soul or death, pure and simple. The latter interpretation is consistent with a physicalist account of the person.[10]

I hope to have shown in my work that an affirmative answer to the question that forms the title of this essay— "Anabaptist science and epistemology?"—is not out of the question. One of the characteristics of modernity—one of its historically conditioned and particular concerns—was the quest for universal, timeless knowledge.[11] Now, at the end of modernity, we can recognize this quest to have been quixotic. But the end of aspirations for universal knowledge need not lead to intellectual chaos; it can instead, as MacIntyre has argued, lead us to recognize our dependence on traditions and to recognize as well that it is only with the resources of a tradition that we can do truly creative intellectual work. I thank all of my predecessors in the Anabaptist tradition for the resources they have provided.

CHAPTER FIVE

Grace as Participation in the Inbreaking of the Kingdom: Mountains of Grace Back Home

Glen H. Stassen

My wife Dot comes from a farm on top of the ridge about ten miles north of Eastern Mennonite University in Harrisonburg, Virginia. From their farm you look west and see green, rolling hills and the mountains of West Virginia. You look east and see the beautiful Shenandoah Valley and the Blue Ridge Mountains. Her father, her brother, and his son have farmed that farm not only for the pigs and the hay, but for the astounding beauty they see every day.

Two years after we married, Dot and I joined with her parents and her brother Bill to take an automobile trip visiting relatives across the Midwest and all the way to Oregon. I had never seen the Rocky Mountains before. They were breathtakingly beautiful. I was ooing and aahing over them when her brother Bill said, "That's not so special. We have mountains like that back home."

I wanted to say, "I hope you realize how special and beautiful are your mountains back home." And that is also what I want to say to Mennonites: I hope you realize how special and beautiful are the mountains you have back home.

I spend my life teaching seminarians and reading Christian ethics books from various traditions. I am convinced that Christendom has developed a tradition of evading the way of Jesus. With the exception of a passage in James McClendon's *Ethics*[1], I challenge you to find a Christian ethics textbook that learns anything constructive from the Sermon on the Mount—the largest block of Jesus' teaching, the teaching that gives us the way of discipleship.

Think of the long tradition that shapes our seeing and acting. Illiteracy was the rule in the Middle Ages; people obtained their understanding of the Christian faith from the art and from the creeds. Go to the Cloisters in New York City, the museum of medieval sculpture and paintings. All that beautiful art has as its subject either Mother Mary and baby Jesus, or Jesus on the cross. Nothing about Jesus' way of discipleship, Jesus' healings and feedings and parables and prophetic teachings, Jesus' way of caring for others. It is like the Apostle's creed: "born of the virgin Mary, crucified under Pontius Pilate. . . ." The way of Jesus Christ and all of his ministry are hidden behind that little comma. Then came the Reformation. Martin Luther split life into two realms: the Sermon on the Mount, he taught, applies only to inner attitudes; you can't guide your actions by Jesus' teachings. Since Luther, Christian practices of economic greed, warmaking, racism, and sexism have influenced the Christian tradition that most have inherited to de-emphasize and ignore—or to praise as "high ideals, impossibly hard teachings"—Jesus' teachings, especially the largest block, the Sermon on the Mount. Is it too much to speak of a tradition of evasion that shapes most Christians?

I hunger and thirst for a tradition that understands, enacts and proclaims Christian discipleship as set forth by Jesus in the Sermon on the Mount. I hope that Mennonites and others in the Anabaptist tradition realize how special is the mountain that they have. The Anabaptist-Mennonite tradition understands, proclaims, and enacts Christian discipleship as set forth by Jesus in the Sermon on the Mount. The Associated Mennonite Biblical Seminary even has a Sermon on the Mount Chapel. Astounding as it sounds, other Christian traditions live in the plains, where they rarely even see the mountain. I want contemporary Mennonites to cele- brate the mountain that they have; to teach it, preach it, enact it, embody it. To spread the word.

Several years ago I had the opportunity to be a researcher on behalf of the National Council of Churches and the Society for Values in Higher Education for a study of model church-related colleges.[2] One college I studied was Goshen College. I was enormously impressed with the faculty, almost all of whom had worked or taught in service or mission proj- ects somewhere abroad, and with the students, most of whom spend a semester in service among needy people in Latin America or elsewhere. The impact of the college on the Christian commitment and service orientation of the students and their values is dramatic. Then I met an African-American Pentecostal student. "Aha!" I thought. "If anyone has experi- enced the less-than-fully-Christian dimensions of Goshen, this double-minority student must be the one. I arranged to have lunch alone with him. But he praised the college, too. After we had developed rapport and trust, I said to him, "Surely there must be something about Goshen College that you would like to change." He answered, "There is one thing: I wish that they would preach what they practice a little more!"

Other colleges, other traditions, would be overjoyed to receive such wonderful, backhanded praise of their practices. Mennonites should appreciate the mountain they have. They should proclaim it articulately, evangelistically. They have a message to spread. They should not assume that other Christians already know about the mountain in their lives.

Recently a call has come from some Mennonites like John Roth, Steve Dintaman, Ted Koontz, Duane Shank, Duane Friesen, and others for a clearer emphasis on grace in Mennonite theology. In 1994 I participated in a wonderful conference at Elizabethtown College on revisioning the Anabaptist vision. Some of the papers from the Elizabethtown conference[3] argued that Harold Bender and John Howard Yoder and the Concerns group have put their emphasis on deeds of discipleship and have neglected the need for grace—the need for a personal relationship with Jesus, the need for the presence of the living Christ, and for the presence of the Holy Spirit in our lives.

I am so loyal to John Howard Yoder that I read that not as criticism—not as a wish to take away from the enormous contribution of Bender, Yoder, and the Concerns group—but as a wish for something additional. I have such powerful appreciation for the practice of discipleship among Mennonites that I hope and pray that this wish does not dilute the beauty and strength of the Mennonite tradition. The need for grace does not mean that Mennonites should adopt some other tradition, whether Lutheran or evangelical or Catholic or pietist or Pentecostal, and substitute it for the mountain they have, although we can all learn something important from each of those traditions, as I know I have. Mennonites do not need to adopt a tradition of cheap grace and cheap faith and abandon the evangelistic mission that they carry, the mission of calling all Christians and non-Christians to follow Jesus concretely.

It takes a lot of chutzpah for a Baptist—even a Baptist with an Anabaptist soul—to suggest to Mennonites how you should interpret the Sermon on the Mount! But I do have a word to spread. I want to celebrate the fact that the Sermon on the Mount is not just human effort or high ideals or hard teachings. The way of Jesus in the Sermon is *the way of deliverance based on grace.*

In this brief space, I want to do a bit of exegesis that Mennonites and other Christians might use to proclaim the Sermon on the Mount as based on grace—as indeed a message of grace, presence, and deliverance.

The central section of the Sermon, beginning with Matt. 5:21, has a consistent pattern of triads, or threefold teachings.

The emphasis in biblical triads comes in the climax, the third member. The central argument that I want to make in the following exegesis is that the climaxes, the third members, are always based in the participative grace of God's loving presence, the grace of God's deliverance from our vicious cycles.[4]

Look first at Matt. 5:23-25. The first part is the *traditional teaching*, from the Ten Commandments: "Thou shalt not kill." The second part is the diagnosis of the *vicious cycle*: being angry with your brother or sister will lead you to be subject to judgment. This is not a high ideal, but a realistic naming of a vicious cycle that we get stuck in. It is not a command, but a participle: being angry. The third part is the climax where the emphasis comes, where the imperatives come: it is *the way of grace* that delivers us from the vicious cycle of anger. Jesus' emphasis is that, when we are angry, we are to go and be reconciled and then come and give thanks in worship. This is participation in the heart of the gospel, the way of grace that God takes toward us in Christ. Something has come between us and God. God does not just give a command from on high. God comes to us in Christ and works out reconciliation. When you go to your brother or sister, you are participating in the way of grace, the way of God toward us in Christ. When you do this, first you pray: "Lord, help me to hear where my brother or sister is coming from; help me to feel his or her feelings; let me picture where he or she is." You practice listening prayer, in which you pray for a sense, a picture, a vision of what your brother or sister cares about. You pray for God's presence in the conversation. You pray that you may follow in the path that Jesus has pioneered, the path of grace, the path that God has taken toward us in Christ.

We need to be clear what we mean by grace. This is not cheap grace—it is not the "grace of the gaps," not the grace of *deus ex machina*, which says God acts only where we do nothing and are passive. Rather, it is *participative* grace. It says God is present, acting this particular way as disclosed in Christ and empowering us to participate in what God is doing. It is delivering grace, delivering us from our vicious cycles. God in Christ comes to us to be reconciled. God in Christ goes to the enemy to work out reconciliation. Participative grace is the grace of participation in the deliverance that God is bringing.

It is not amorphous grace, trusting in God in a vague way. It has specific shape: God acts these particular ways in Jesus Christ, and is acting in these ways now; we are invited, called, to participate in this *Christomorphic* grace in ways that fit the shape of what God is doing.

Or consider Matt. 39b-42. Here again we have a *traditional teaching*, "an eye for an eye. . . ." And we have a diagnosis of a *vicious cycle*: the kind of resistance that is retaliatory, vengeful or violent or by evil means.[5] That is why Paul paraphrases it in Romans 12:19ff., "Never avenge yourselves. . . . Do not be overcome by evil, but overcome evil with good."

Again, the emphasis comes in the climax, the third member of the teaching, *the way of grace and deliverance*, which offers four transforming initiatives of peacemaking: *turning* the other cheek, *giving* your coat, *going* the second mile, *giving* to the one who begs. These strategies represent not merely "giving in," but they are truly transforming initiatives of peacemaking, the kind that Gandhi and King taught. In them we not only die to violence but we are also raised to initiatives of peacemaking. They are nonviolent ways of confronting injustice and domination; they assert another way of relating, a way of peace and justice; they invite humans to a new relationship of mutual respect and shalom.

Ulrich Luz points out that these initiatives are formulated to shock, to surprise, to draw a direct contrast with usual behavior in the world. They are a deliberate protest and a reversal of normal behavior.

> Thus they are indirectly determined by the arrival of the kingdom of God. That fits well into the eschatology of Jesus, who again and again speaks . . . of the everyday life which is influenced by the kingdom of God (as in the parables). . . . For Jesus, the arrival of the kingdom of God is manifested as limit-

less love of God for the people, which makes possible the love of humans among themselves and even for their enemies.

They are participating in the grace of the kingdom of God.[6]

Walter Grundmann, in a study that has not been widely noticed, argues insightfully that the whole Sermon on the Mount seems to be organized to correspond with the petitions of the Lord's Prayer.[7] The beatitudes celebrate the coming of the kingdom. They articulate the first petition: "Thy kingdom come." They are blessings, celebrations. We are blessed because we get to participate in the grace of the coming of the kingdom. The six triads of Matt. 5:21-48 correlate to the petition, "Thy will be done on earth as it is in heaven." And here is the key: In the Lord's prayer, God's will is not first of all what we do, but is first of all what God does, and is doing now ("Thy will be done"), just as "thy kingdom come" is not first of all what we do, but what God is doing and will do. The Lord's Prayer is a prayer for God to bring the deliverance, for God's kingdom to come, for God to give us our daily bread and forgive us and deliver us from temptation. Here Jesus shows how God's deliverance, God's will, God's love, is happening in our midst. Taking these transforming initiatives toward our enemies is participating in the deliverance God brings in Christ.

Notice also that the four initiatives that Jesus teaches here use seven of the same Greek words in the Septuagint version of the Suffering Servant passage, Isaiah 50:4-9: resist, slap, cheek, sue, coat, give, and turn away. Isaiah 50:4-9 is a passage of participative grace, in which God, the Lord, gives deliverance and the servant's actions participate in that deliverance:

> The Lord God has given me the tongue of a teacher, that I may know how to sustain the weary with a word. Morning by morning he wakens—wakens my ear to listen as those who are taught.... I gave my back to those who struck me, and my cheeks to those who pulled out the beard; I did not hide my face from insult and spitting. The Lord God helps me; therefore

I have not been disgraced; therefore I have set my face like flint, and I know that I shall not be put to shame; he who vindicates me is near.... It is the Lord God who helps me; who will declare me guilty?

Furthermore, each of the four initiatives seems to look forward to Jesus' crucifixion and suggests our participation in Jesus' way of the cross. Davies and Allison write: "Jesus himself was struck and slapped (26:67: *rapidzo*) and his garments (27:35: *himatia*) were taken from him. If his followers then turn the other cheek and let the enemy have their clothes, will they not be remembering their Lord, especially in his passion?"[8] And the word "compels," as in "if someone *compels* you to go one mile," is the Greek word used when Simon of Cyrene is *compelled* to carry Jesus' cross, thus participating in Jesus' crucifixion with him (Matt. 27:32). Jesus gives his life for us. When we go the second mile as an initiative of peacemaking, when we give to the poor, we are participating in the way of Jesus who was crucified for us. We are participating in the grace of the cross.

I have experienced a double encounter with grace in the context of nonviolent confrontation of the enemy. In the 1980s my friend Andreas Zumach of the Christian alternative service organization in West Germany, Action Reconciliation/ Peace Service, was traveling regularly to Poland and East Germany to teach the practices of nonviolent direct action that he had learned from Cesar Chavez and Martin Luther King during his own alternative service among the migrant laborers in California. The writings of Martin Luther King were translated into German, and groups were studying them in churches. I saw the writings and saw the pictures of Dr. King in the churches and knew the connection between the way of Jesus and the strategies of the peace movement there. People told me how they would pray at each of the meetings that the demonstrations would be nonviolent. At the end of my trip there with some of my students in 1987, we met in a church basement for coffee and *Kuchen*. The meeting ended with a round of spontaneous prayers by the East

German Baptists and by us American Baptists. My students and I were deeply moved by the fervency and gratitude of the prayers of the East German Baptists, true to their pietist tradition. In 1989 I was there again when these methods of nonviolent action were crucial in the turning from violence to nonviolence, and when the harsh dictator Eric Honecker was toppled and the Wall was opened. They were singing "We Shall Overcome" in English! Overcome by God's grace, I wept.[9]

Later, back in the U.S., I was confronted several times, nonviolently, for the drivenness of my type A, resentful heart. I was also confronted by the gratitude of the members testifying in worship at Canaan Baptist Church of Christ, by an action of grace that saved me from a horrendous accident, by a very good friend who spoke directly, by a counselor who spoke equally directly, by my wife's loving encouragement, and by Joyce Hollyday's Bible study at the Baptist Peace Fellowship summer conference. It takes a lot of nonviolent confrontation to get through my thick heart! At the conference, I went off and practiced listening prayer, asking God what change I should make and entered in a journal a commitment to a kind of discipleship I should have committed to long before. Then in the evening worship service Ken Sehested, the Executive Director of the Baptist Peace Fellowship, asked me to pray in German, as others prayed in other languages. It made me remember those fervent prayers by the East German Baptists. I prayed fervently for a turning in my heart, a cleansing from resentment and for a heart open to gratitude. During the worship service, several of my former students surprised me by presenting me an outrageously funny gift of gratitude. Suddenly, my heart was indeed turned from resentment to gratitude. It was a life-saving change, and it has lasted.[10] Think of all the different kinds of actions that contributed to this experience of grace and turning: nonviolent direct action, confrontation, loving support, confession of sin, new commitment, and a gift from those I care about. Jesus taught all these forms of grace, and they all happened to me.

Look at Matt. 5:44-45: "But I say to you, Love your enemies and pray for those who persecute you, so that you may
be children of your Father in heaven; for he makes his sun
rise on the evil and on the good, and sends rain on the righteous and on the unrighteous." Here it could not be clearer
that loving our enemy and praying for our enemy are ways
of participating in God's grace: we are children of our Father
who is in heaven. For God makes the sun rise on the evil and
on the good, and sends rain on the just and on the unjust.
God is already there, bestowing grace on our enemy. God is
already here, bestowing grace on me a sinner—I who have
done evil that I know too well; I who have been unjust in
ways that my comfortable social situation has hidden from
my awareness. When I love my enemy and pray for my
enemy, I am participating in the gracious blessing that God is
giving every day. And I am participating in Jesus' action of
forgiving his enemies who crucified him, not knowing what
they were doing. Jesus' disciples betrayed him and would
not stand by him. That is our part in the drama: we betray
him and fail to stand by him, yet Jesus forgives us as he for-
gave them, and Jesus gives us the ministry of feeding his
sheep as he gave that ministry to Peter (Jn. 21:15ff.).

The concluding verse, "Be perfect, therefore, as your heavenly Father is perfect" (Mt. 5:48), is not about moral perfection. In biblical language you can't say, "as God is morally
perfect." The "therefore" points back to God's including enemies in the grace of sunshine and rain. It means that you
should be all-inclusive in your love, as participants in the
grace that your heavenly Father gives to enemies. Luke 6:35-
36 is clear: ". . . you will be children of the Most High; for he
is kind to the ungrateful and the wicked. Be merciful, just as
your Father is merciful." This is not about moral perfection
and works-righteousness, but about participating in God's
gracious, all-inclusive, delivering love.

In all of these teachings, God's love is the interpretive key.
Chapter 5 has its summation and climax here with God's love
for just and unjust alike—God's all-inclusive, grace-filled

love. The whole central section of the Sermon has its summation and climax with the Golden Rule. In Matthew 7:12 and 22:37-40 Jesus tells us that the whole Law and the Prophets hinge on love. Mercy is central in Matthew.[11]

Again we have a traditional teaching in "No one can serve two masters; . . . . You cannot serve God and wealth" (Mt. 6:24-33). And we have the diagnosis of a vicious cycle: worrying about possessions, about what we shall eat and what we shall wear, instead of trusting God. The transforming initiative is to invest ourselves and our money in seeking first God's reign and God's justice. God's kingdom is all about God's grace, about God's bringing deliverance on earth as in heaven, and about God's making us blessed by making us participants in God's bringing the deliverance of God's reign. The passages in the prophets and the psalms that foretell the reign of God regularly have four marks: the light of God's *presence*; the joy of God's *salvation*; the relief of God's *peacemaking*; and the deliverance of God's delivering, community-restoring *justice*. Investing ourselves in God's reign and God's justice is participating in the deliverance and community of God's reign, God's kingdom. It is participation in grace.[12]

At the end of the Sermon on the Mount we find once again an expression of the transforming initiative of participation in God's grace: "Ask, and it will be given you; search, and you will find; knock, and the door will be opened for you. . . . If you then, who are evil, know how to give good gifts to your children, how much more will your Father in heaven give good gifts to those who ask him!" Moreover, as God gives to us, so should we give to others: "In everything do to others as you would have them do to you" (Mt. 7:6-12). The Golden Rule is based on God's grace of giving gifts: our giving to others is participating in God's gracious way of giving to us.

Duane Friesen, in his book, *Artists, Citizens, Philosophers: Seeking the Peace of the City: An Anabaptist Theology of Culture,* [13] paraphrases and quotes from something that I wrote. I include this lengthy quote because I want to call attention to

Friesen's book, which gives incisive guidance for gospel transformation of our lives in the cities where we dwell. But his quote also captures what I am trying to say more accurately, concisely, and better than I could say it myself:

> Matthew's Sermon on the Mount is not about abstract ideals that are difficult or impossible to implement. The sermon consists of a series of fourteen imperatives or transforming initiatives made possible by God's delivering grace that are concrete, practical, and doable. One of these imperatives is the call to prayer.
>
> It is striking how often prayer is discussed in the Sermon on the Mount. . . . Prayer comes up three times in the Sermon: the imperative to pray for our enemies and those who persecute us (Matt. 5:44); imperatives about how to pray, including [praying in secret] and the Lord's Prayer (Matt. 6:5-13); and the imperative to make one's requests known to God (Matt. 7:6-11). . . . "Prayer is asking God's delivering grace to happen; and it is participating in the grace and deliverance." It includes facing the evil that is in us. It is not only speaking, but also listening to the Spirit of God praying in us. In the Lord's Prayer we pray for God's rule (the transforming power of God's justice and peace) to come on earth "as it is in heaven." And in the second section of the prayer, we pray "for God to deliver us from four concrete threats—hunger, debt, temptation, and evil . . . (Matt. 6:11-13)." Prayer is not a substitute for action. Rather, it places human action and responsibility within the framework of God's transforming power. Martin Luther King expresses the fundamental meaning of prayer with his conviction that, in the struggle for justice, humans have cosmic companionship.

The whole Gospel of Matthew and the Sermon on the Mount are about the presence of God. Ulrich Luz[14] points out insightfully that the Gospel of Matthew begins by saying that the name of Jesus is Emmanuel—God with us. And Matthew ends with, "I am with you always, to the end of the age." The theme of God's presence in Jesus recurs again and again throughout the Gospel. Jesus proclaims the kingdom, which is the presence of God. Repeatedly Jesus teaches that "your

Father who sees in secret" (Mt. 6:4, 6, 18). Your Father knows what you need before you ask him" (6:8). Your heavenly Father gives rain and sunshine to the just and unjust. Your Father feeds the birds of the air and clothes the lilies of the field. Your Father gives good things to those who ask.

Martin Luther King tells of the time of the dark night of the soul, when he despaired of the struggle. The key to the turning for him was a time of intense prayer in his kitchen, when the delivering grace of God came clearly to him. And then, said King, after the dark night came the dawn of hope.

I do not want to compare myself with Martin Luther King, but I do want to give my witness. There have been some overwhelming turning points in my life—times when God's grace has turned me from despair to hope, or from unfaithfulness to repentance, or has turned my heart from resentment to gratitude. Sometimes the turning points have come when someone has confronted me with brotherly or sisterly admonition, or when the dark night of defeat has caused me to face my own limits and the limits of the sinful world in which we live. But the grace has almost always come in the midst of fervent prayer in the presence of God. Often it has been listening prayer, when I am silent in the presence of God, letting those concerns that well up be placed before God, and listening for what God will say or what vision God will give.

I believe deeply that the disciple who will live by the way of Jesus in the Sermon on the Mount will live in the presence of the God of grace, who knows our concerns in secret, who is present to us even when we are not aware of it, who is present to us in our praying, who does give us gracious guidance, and who turns us from self-righteousness and resentment to gratitude. Is this presence of God perhaps what non-charismatics have to learn from Pentecostalism, which is spreading in many places, as Anabaptism spread rapidly in the sixteenth century, emphasizing the presence of God in the midst of our lives? Is the presence of God one thing non-sacramentalists have to learn from Catholics, with their sense of the presence of Christ in the Mass? Is the sense of the gracious presence of God an important reality to give thanks for in the midst of our various ministries and service projects?

I'm just a lowly Baptist, a benefactor from the crumbs fallen off the table of the great tradition of the Anabaptists. I don't know why I should be writing for Mennonites. But coming from the lowlands as I do, I want to encourage Mennonites to give God thanks for the beautiful mountains you have in Anabaptist tradition. Don't slight that tradition in search of some cheap-grace tradition that talks about grace without participating in God's gracious reign, God's kingdom, the way of Jesus Christ, the Sermon on the Mount. Mennonites do not need to go somewhere else in search of the mountain. They should rather give thanks for the beauty of the awesome mountains they already have. They should teach and preach the way of *Nachfolge Christi*, the way of following Jesus. And teach and preach the way of Jesus as the way of participating in the grace of the inbreaking of God's kingdom.

I pray for the blessings of God's participative grace on Mennonites and on the Anabaptist-Mennonite witness to the world.

CHAPTER SIX

Latin America and Anabaptist Theology

Samuel Escobar

As a Peruvian missionary to university students in Argentina during the 1960s I experienced the ecstasy and the agony of revolutionary times. The air was filled with revolutionary songs, the socialist utopia seemed to be waiting for us at the turn of the corner and Che Guevara, the Argentinean medical doctor turned romantic guerrilla fighter in Cuba, was the hero for large crowds of enthusiastic young people. Christians had a tremendous sense of urgency about defining their role in a changing society. The mood is well reflected in the first chapter of a classic book about the development of liberation theology in those years. It opens with a conversation with author José Míguez Bonino and a group of young people in Uruguay: "... somebody asked the question, 'Who then is Jesus Christ?' 'For us,' one of the group shot back immediately and spontaneously, 'Jesus Christ is Che Guevara.'"[1] Reflecting on that outburst, Míguez Bonino wrote that one of its meanings could well be: "What we discover in Guevara is linked with the name of Jesus Christ . . . in other words: liberation and revolution are a legitimate transcription of the Gospel."[2]

In such an atmosphere, and with fear and trembling, the evangelical student group and the periodical *Certeza* that I edited invited John Howard Yoder to speak about "Revolution and Christian Ethics" in Cordoba, Argentina. At that time in 1970 he had been lecturing as a visiting professor at the Mennonite Seminary in Montevideo, Uruguay, and at ISEDET (Union Seminary) in Buenos Aires, Argentina. A large crowd of students, pastors and Christian leaders filled the main auditorium of the downtown Methodist Church where he spoke. Yoder had taught himself Spanish and he spoke it with a slightly French accent, but he communicated with ease and carried on a two-hour dialogue with avid questions from the audience. I transcribed the lecture and published it the following year.[3] The text very much follows the structure of "The Original Revolution," the initial chapter of Yoder's book by the same title, which announced some of the themes developed later in *The Politics of Jesus*.

That evening after the lecture in Cordoba my wife Lilly and I had Yoder as a guest at our home, and in a long Argentinean after-dinner conversation that lasted beyond midnight, we came to know a bit about his life and ideas. He told us of his five years with MCC in postwar France and his studies under Barth and Cullman. It was the beginning of a long and much appreciated friendship which enriched my own Christian experience and theology as well as that of a generation of evangelicals in the Latin American Theological Fraternity (LATF), which was founded a few weeks later, in December of that year, in Cochabamba, Bolivia.[4] LATF was partly an outcome of the First Latin American Congress of Evangelism (CLADE I) held in Bogota, Colombia, in December of 1969. As founders of LATF we were trying to respond to the challenges of the revolutionary moment in Latin America by being faithful to our evangelical heritage but also relevant to the critical moments our countries were facing.

Yoder and the Latin American Theological Fraternity

The paper I presented at CLADE I about "The Social Responsibility of the Church in Latin America" was later published in English and brought invitations to speak at several evangelical gatherings in those years.[5] Two elements of my own reflection became the point of connection with Anabaptist theology. First, that when Christian presence in the world is patterned by the example of Jesus Christ according to the Scriptures, it becomes socially relevant because it is transformative. Second, that our experience as Protestant minorities in culturally Roman Catholic societies gives us a unique ground for perceiving both the decline of Christendom and the radically transformative nature of the Gospel. I still recall the exhilaration I experienced in readings and conversations with Yoder as he provided us vistas into the rich horizon of Anabaptist thought. As a Baptist, I was discovering a hidden Anabaptist heritage that Baptist missionaries from the U.S. had never made explicit and relevant. Even most Mennonites I had met in Argentina were not aware of key tenets of the Anabaptist tradition that were prominent in Yoder's position.

For an evangelical who valued highly the authority of scripture, I found Yoder's approach attractive because it took the text seriously in its integrity and offered a way of reading it "in its own terms." Any careful reader of *The Original Revolution* or *The Politics of Jesus* is also aware that, besides work with the text itself, Yoder's approach was informed by a sociological understanding of the church today as well as with the church depicted in the New Testament. This sociological awareness is clear, not in scholarly quotations from sociologists, but in the way Yoder analyzed history and institutions. Yoder's reading of scripture was also rooted in awareness of a tradition that has intentionally aimed to practice a form of discipleship that dares to question the accepted wisdom of so-called Christian societies. However, Yoder was not arrogant or complacent about the Mennonite tradition he represented.[6] He found parallels between the experience of Protestant minorities in Latin America and Mennonites in their "peculiar people" experience as a minority in Europe and North America.

Yoder, who was invited to become a member of LATF, presented a paper at its Second Consultation in Lima in 1972. The theme was "The Kingdom of God" and Yoder's contribution was "The Messianic Expectation of the Kingdom and its Centrality for an Adequate Contemporary Hermeneutics." As I worked with him in the editing of his Spanish text, he insisted on this long title for the sake of precision. My own paper for the consultation was on the Kingdom of God and social and political ethics.[7] In that paper I analyzed our Protestant experience, using some elements from Franklin Littell's approach.[8] My thesis was that Latin American Protestants had an Anabaptist stance even if their theology was not directly connected to Anabaptist missionary or literary sources. Consequently, we needed to delve into the richness of the Anabaptist heritage as we tried to define our identity and work on a contextual theology.

During the consultation in Lima one of the hotly debated issues was the relationship of churches to political structures. Some participants from Brazil made eloquent apologies for the cooperation of Protestants with the rightist military junta in power in their country. They clashed with participants from Chile who were enthusiastic supporters of Salvador Allende's socialist experiment. Both parties tried to formulate a theological explanation for their stance. At a couple of points Yoder called us to reflection. Instead of patriotic defenders of our respective Caesars, shouldn't we be helping one another to know how to be better witnesses to them? His simple, dispassionate way of asking embarrassing, basic questions brought more than one fiery debate to a point of reflective silence.

After this consultation Yoder became a key interlocutor and fellow pilgrim for the members of LATF, even for those who did not accept some points of his Anabaptist perspective. His writings became influential, although, regrettably, publication of the Spanish edition of The Politics of Jesus was not possible until 1985.[9] Semilla-Clara, the Anabaptist publishers in Spanish, have since made available several of his other books and writings.

Yoder and the Lausanne Movement

In 1974 American evangelist Billy Graham and several evangelical missionary and evangelistic organizations convened the Lausanne Congress on Evangelism in an effort to coordinate and foster missionary efforts on a global scale. Missionary activism by mainline Protestant denominations had declined after World War II, but there was an explosion of evangelical and independent missionary agencies. Lausanne 1974 was an opportunity to evaluate that activism. What some conveners and organizers planned as a great celebration and a time to teach American missionary wisdom to the rest of the world became instead a time for sobering, self-critical reflection.[10] The consensus reached during the Congress is summarized in the "Lausanne Covenant," one of the great missiological documents of the twentieth century. Evangelicals from different parts of the world were able to bring the issue of social responsibility to the missiological agenda of western evangelicalism. They insisted that the quality of the Christian presence in the world is as important as—or even more important than—the amount of missionary work and the orthodoxy of the message.

The Lausanne Covenant expressed well the repentance for what theologian René Padilla called "unbiblical" dichotomies separating proclamation of the *kerygma* from *diakonia*, *didache* and *koinonia*.[11] As a member of the program committee that organized Lausanne under Leighton Ford's leadership, I had recommended the inclusion of John Howard Yoder in the Congress. He attended and teamed up with Latin Americans, Europeans, and Australians to work on the "Response to Lausanne." This was a kind of "radical evangelical" comment on or supplement to the Lausanne Covenant, regarding points where some participants felt that the Covenant had not gone far enough. Even before Lausanne, Yoder had been involved in theological evaluation of the "Church Growth" movement, which strongly opposed the radical evangelicals at Lausanne.[12]

In 1977 Yoder was asked to be "a brotherly commentator

on content and process" during the Third Consultation of LATF in Itaici, Brazil. Yoder called us to reflect on how our Latin male chauvinism showed in spite of our loud endorsement of New Testament ethics and discipleship. For the LATF twentieth anniversary celebration in Quito (December 1990) Yoder presented a paper on "Violence and Non-violence."[13] Our reflection agenda was a review of twenty years of activity, focusing on issues that had been the subject of continued action, research and writing: violence and non-violence; poverty and stewardship; oppression and justice; authoritarianism and power. Evangelical participation in social and political movements called now for a theological "reflection on praxis." Some of us were convinced of the need for an extended dialogue between the Reformed and Anabaptist traditions within the Latin American context. While Yoder agreed on the need to formulate some kind of evangelical social ethics, he emphasized that it was most important for us at that point to deal with the pastoral issues posed by social and political activism.

I had the privilege of participating in the Thanksgiving Workshop that Ron Sider and several evangelical leaders convened in the Chicago YMCA late in November 1973. At the time I was working in Canada as director of Inter Varsity Christian Fellowship. Yoder was one of the contributors to the intense dialogue of the workshop which produced the "Chicago Declaration of Evangelical Social Concern" and, later on, the birth of Evangelicals for Social Action under the leadership of Ron Sider. After the workshop I traveled with Yoder to Reba Place near Evanston, where I met Virgil Vogt and shared for a day in the life of one of the oldest Anabaptist intentional communities in the U.S. Then we drove to Elkhart where I stayed at Yoder's home and visited the Associated Biblical Seminaries as well as Goshen College. Acquaintance developed into friendship with men such as Cornelius Dyck, who later invited me to lecture at the Institute for Mennonite Studies. The lectures were published in book form, along with a chapter by John Driver.[14]

While working as a theological educator in Latin America, John Driver was also active in LATF. During warm and extended dialogues John made us aware of ecclesiological and pastoral dimensions of the Anabaptist heritage that were sometimes briefly outlined or suggested in Yoder's writings. During my doctoral studies in Spain I found myself in contact with the numerous Plymouth Brethren assemblies that had developed as part of the tiny Protestant minority in that country. Some aspects of Brethren ecclesiology connect naturally with Anabaptist ecclesiology. Thus, when John Driver went to work in Spain he initially cooperated with the Brethren. That was at the end of the dictatorial regime of Francisco Franco, when a nearly medieval society rapidly became liberal and secular. Driver and I found ourselves teaching together in Madrid during the 1977 Annual Conference of the Assemblies. Innumerable questions about leadership styles, order, and democracy in the life of the church presented themselves. Driver presented a series about the nature of the church and I did a parallel one about the mission of the church. Both of us tried to deal with the difficult pastoral questions raised by elders of the Assemblies during closed breakfast sessions.

As I look back at the past three decades of evangelical theological reflection in Latin America, clearly Anabaptist theology has been one of the most fertile sources for our contextual approach. As part of a growing religious minority within a post-Christendom culture, evangelical pastors, missionaries, and theological educators have been involved in a search for answers to new pastoral and missiological questions. We have been forced to look for a new way of doing theology. As I have said elsewhere, on the one hand "ecumenical theology from Geneva was shaped by a mood and a stance that reflected the uncertainties and the fatigue of a declining Protestantism in Europe." And on the other hand "liberation theology from Catholic sources was heavily dependent on the assumption that Latin America was 'a Christian continent.'"[15] In that predicament, Yoder's creative reading of scripture became a valuable gift. His writings prompted new questions and suggested new routes for reconsidering the relevance of New Testament paradigms for Christian mission today. I will focus on that aspect of his work in the second part of this essay. While at first sight it may appear that Anabaptist thought has provided insights, frames, and metaphors for developments in social ethics, I am now convinced that eventually we will find its most durable impact on ecclesiological and missiological action and reflection.

Mission within a Creative Tension

Questions about Christian mission were not absent from Yoder's theology. This explains why he could actively and intentionally connect with evangelical theologians in Latin America for whose reflection the missiological agenda was central and decisive. They could not conceive of their existence in Latin America as other than a missionary presence. Actually, since the early 1960s Yoder had been writing about missionary issues as is evident, for instance, in some of his writings for *Concern*, "A Pamphlet Series for Questions of Christian Renewal," and in his work as a consultant for the Mennonite Board of Missions.

Here I want to emphasize two premises of Yoder's reflection. First, his understanding that

> the Anabaptist vision calls for a Believers' Church. With reference to the outside this means that the Church is by definition missionary . . . is a church which invites men into fellowship. Men and women who were not born into that fellowship are invited to enter it by free adult decision in response to the proclamation of the love and suffering of God.[16]

Second, his premise that "there might be about the biblical vision of reality certain dimensions which refuse to be pushed into the mold of any one contemporary worldview, but which stand in creative tension with the cultural functions of our age or perhaps of any age."[17] The church is the community that lives by the biblical vision. The church proclaims that the existence of the universe and human history can only be understood and make sense within the purpose of God as manifested in Jesus Christ by the power of the Holy Spirit. "With the coming of Jesus Christ all barriers that divide humankind have been broken down and a new humanity is now taking shape *in* and *through* the church."[18] Because the church sees its own existence as the fulfillment of that biblical vision and lives by it, she should therefore be a community that embodies that creative tension with all the contradictions and agonies involved.

The history of missions includes transitional moments when missionaries become the prophetic voice that stands at the center of that "creative tension," embodying in their persons the dilemmas and agonies of a life between the times. Take, for instance, the classical example of the apostle Paul. Yoder has been among those New Testament interpreters who remind us that a correct understanding of Pauline writings should always take into account their missiological context. Thus, for instance, the writings of Paul to the Corinthians should not be read "as if they were meant to be sources of finely coined phrases ready to be integrated into a system of theology" nor "as a series of statements about the self-understanding of the believer as he sees his life in the light of faith."[19] Paul's writings, Yoder insisted, should be taken for what they actually were in their origins: missionary correspondence by a missionary who had planted some churches that needed to learn how to be the church in a pagan world. "He cares especially about the problems of being a missionary church which proclaims and incarnates a Jewish message in a Gentile world."[20]

We grasp better the thrust of Pauline teachings within their missionary context when the theological search for their meaning comes from a missionary situation rather than merely from academic curiosity. Take, for instance, the issue of the alleged social conservatism of Paul that has been proposed by some ethicists and taken for granted by others.

Such conservatism becomes embarrassing and even scandalous in missionary situations where the daily life of the church is affected by blatant injustices. Paul's apparent silence about slavery or, even worse, his appeasing calls to submission in the *Haustafeln*, lend themselves to the accusation of "demobilizing the poor," as a liberation theologian would say. Yoder has analyzed how some ethicists, who read the Pauline texts from the perspective of a Constantinian status quo, have interpreted Paul providing corrections to "the apparent social radicality of Jesus himself."[21] They presupposed that the practice of Jesus could not be the basis of an ethical construct outside his immediate Palestinian context.

By careful analysis of biblical texts, Yoder proves that it is possible to argue consistently for the possibility of a messianic ethic that makes sense in our time. His work also opens the door for a missiological reformation that takes seriously the examples of Jesus and Paul as patterns for mission today. Yoder developed an exegetical path that established a close link between the practice and the teaching of both Jesus and Paul and grasped the meaning of the teachings, not only in light of the cultural and historical context but also in light of the missionary practice of Jesus and his apostle. In *The Politics of Jesus* Yoder was explicit about his program: "I shall be looking more at the events than at the teachings, more at the outlines than at the substance."[22] And he has also followed it creatively in other writings. Yoder's exegesis of the Pauline material is captured in the expression "revolutionary subordination." Paul's teaching was consistent with his own missionary practice, which in fact:

> derives from the example and the teaching of Jesus himself.
> . . . His motto of revolutionary subordination, of willing servanthood in the place of domination, enables the person in a subordinate position in society to accept and live within that status without resentment, at the same time that it calls upon the person in the superordinate position to forsake or renounce all domineering use of his status.[23]

Yoder's reference to Pauline missionary practice and teaching derives from Jesus' own practice and teaching that has been an important factor in theological development in Latin America. I have described it elsewhere as the search for a missiological Christology that takes very seriously the soteriological Christology of the evangelical missionary movement, but also goes beyond it.[24] René Padilla has insisted on the eschatological and soteriological dimensions of the Christian message centered in the person of Jesus Christ. In him, through the pattern of promise and fulfillment, the Old and New Testaments are related. From a careful exposition of the Gospel centered around a solid Christological core, Padilla concludes that "the apostolic mission is derived from Jesus Christ. He is the content as well as the model and the goal for the proclamation of the gospel."[25]

One consequence of this search is a critical evaluation of the extreme individualism of those missiologies that have lost the biblical wholeness: "The salvation that the Gospel proclaims is not limited to man's reconciliation to God. It involves the remaking of man in all the dimensions of his existence. It has to do with the recovery of the whole man according to God's original purpose for his creation."[26] This holistic dimension of the Gospel allows us to understand the New Testament teaching about the nature of human beings, which is offered within a missiological context. This constitutes an important safeguard against the pitfalls of hermeneutical procedures that read the values of our contemporary culture into the text. On the basis of this biblical teaching, Yoder as well as Padilla evaluated critically the "Homogeneous Unit Principle" proposed by American missiologists of the Church Growth school.[27] This understanding has become especially relevant as racism becomes one of the most difficult issues that missionary work faces in the twenty-first century.

In his study of 2 Cor. 5:17, Yoder offers an excellent example of the corrective return to reading a text within its missiological context. He offers his own translation of this text: "If anyone is in Christ, then God creates anew."[28] The "newness" that Paul is proclaiming is closely connected with his own missionary work as a Jew who happens to be a missionary to Gentiles: "He does not perceive people as Jew or Greek, but as the new people whom they have become in Christ. Because Christ has taken the place of all, now all persons can be seen in the image of Christ."[29] Precisely what Paul is doing is founding churches, communities of new people who express the novelty taught by the Gospel. The newness cannot be perceived in isolated individual believers: "The reconciliation of Jew and Gentile in the 'new humanity' is *first* a community event. It cannot happen to a lone individual. The prerequisite for personal change is a new context into which to enter. A Gentile can only find Abraham by meeting a Jew. A Jew can only celebrate the messianic age by welcoming a Gentile."[30]

Mission from the Periphery

In a pamphlet published in 1961 Yoder is surprisingly aware of trends that were affecting missionary work but that were perceived by most missiologists only two decades later. In 1961, Yoder said: "One extremely significant recent development—worth a pamphlet in its own right—is the participation of non-Western churches in missionary sending with Japanese going to Brazil or India, Indonesians to the Pacific Islands, Brazilians to Angola."[31] This trend increased significantly in the last decades of the twentieth century, within the frame of what missiologist Andrew Walls has described as "a massive southward shift of the center of gravity of the Christian world, so that the representative Christian lands now appear to be in Latin America, sub-Saharan Africa, and other parts of the southern continents."[32] The existence of thriving churches in what used to be called the Third World confronts the old European or North American churches with a new set of questions and new ways of looking at God's Word.

The theological agenda is shifting because new pastoral

situations and theological questions are coming from churches in the frontier between Christendom and Islam, churches surrounded by cultures shaped by animism or great ethnic religions, ethnic churches in the impoverished heart of secularized Western cities, thriving Pentecostal churches in Latin America, or old churches in post-Marxist Eastern Europe. These are the missionary churches of today and tomorrow, and, in addition to being attentive to the Word of God, the ears of the missiologists should be tuned to their message, their songs, and their groans. New missionary patterns are developing, and part of the agenda for theological reflection in the future will be to find out how understanding this new situation can become part of a coherent missiology with a global thrust.

By 1984 Yoder remarked, "It is one of the widely remarked developments of our century that now one dimension, now another, of the ecclesiastical experience and the ecclesiological vision once called 'sectarian' are now beginning to be espoused by some within majority communions."[33] Perhaps as Christians and churches search for more faithful patterns of missionary obedience to Jesus Christ, they increasingly find themselves being disestablished in societies that hold some form of "official" Christian identity. They discover, like "sectarians" of the past, that they must learn to live as "resident aliens."

On the other hand, out of his experience in Latin America and among the Latino minority churches in North America, Orlando Costas worked at the development of a missiology that would express the experience of churches on "the periphery," far from the center of political, financial, and technological power. Costas used what he called the "Galilean model" to interpret the missionary engagement of these churches in their own societies and their involvement in mission at a global scale. Concentrating on the Gospel of Mark, Costas explored a model of evangelization rooted in the ministry of Jesus. He characterized it as an evangelistic legacy, "a model of contextual evangelization from the periphery."[34] He placed special significance on Jesus' choice of Galilee, a racial and cultural crossroads, as the base for his mission. He also explored the significance of Jesus' identity as a Galilean, and of Galilee as an evangelistic landmark and the starting point of the mission to the nations with its universal implications. Costas' understanding of his own contemporary context emphasized the "peripheral" nature of some of the points and places where Christianity is more dynamic today.

At some point the "sectarian" vision to which Yoder referred—coming, as it did, from the periphery of official Catholic and Protestant versions of history—may have a fertile encounter with the theological questions coming from missionary churches in the peripheries of the contemporary world. Paraphrasing Yoder, we could say that new "community events" will be necessary in the reconciliation of Christians from the North and Christians from the South, as they experience what it means to become a "new humanity," and as they theologize about it.

CHAPTER SEVEN

Anabaptism and Radical Christianity

Christopher Rowland

In reflecting on this essay I find myself returning to a task several of us in the United Kingdom engaged in a couple of years ago.[1] We were asked to discuss what attracted us to the Anabaptist tradition. We did so in order to offer a narrative approach to the theological task rightly underlined by Jim McClendon in his systematic theology.

My story goes back to 1987, when in the middle of doing the preparatory reading for a book on radical Christianity,[2] I journeyed to the London Mennonite Centre and met twentieth-century Anabaptists. I discovered there that Anabaptism was not a phenomenon confined to the pages of church history books but a real living Christian practice. That year I began a friendship with Alan and Eleanor Kreider. They have sustained me and guided me and helped me see that the pattern of Christian discipleship—which for such a long time I, a life-long Anglican, had thought no one shared with me— was in fact shared by thousands of others around the world. I realized that my inchoate commitment to pacifism and an egalitarian church structure, and my approach to biblical wisdom, were also part of other Christians' vision of discipleship then and now. I found people who thought that the sayings of Jesus in the Sermon on the Mount were meant to inform and influence life in the contemporary world and were a central constituent of practical discipleship; who were not only committed to peace but to finding the means whereby it could be implemented; who had a healthy suspicion of the state and its ideology; and who gave a high priority to practical discipleship as the necessary context for understanding Christian faith. Theologically and spiritually, I had found a "home" in the twentieth century. I no longer had to be a spiritual exile who could only look back to the ideas of the Diggers (Christian radicals of the English Civil War period after the execution of Charles I in 1649) or the Anabaptists of yesteryear. I could find them today, informing theology and contemporary commitments to justice and peace. I have learned much from friends in the Anabaptist tradition like Alan and Eleanor Kreider, both of whom I consider my guides and mentors as well as close friends. But I have also gained wisdom and insight from Jim McClendon, whom I have come to know in recent years, whose original approach to systematic theology I applaud and from whose insight, wisdom, and encouragement I have derived great benefit.[3]

My growing interest in Anabaptism coincided with my conversion to liberation theology.[4] Since that confluence may not be typical for all those who have been influenced by Anabaptism, I should explain the connections. Two things struck me forcibly about my initial experience of the Christian practice of the Basic Ecclesial Communities (CEB) in Brazil twenty years ago. First I recognized the inescapably narrative foundation of Christian theology as the stories of Scripture, especially that of Jesus Christ, interacted with and informed contemporary stories. That tradition of testimonies of discipleship is an important part of Anabaptist theologizing; contemporary life-experiences are part of that ongoing activity of the spirit of Jesus and a guide to understanding the ancient testimonies of those who were disciples. This element is evident every time one participates in a grassroots community study in Latin America and hears it stressed that there are two texts: the text of "life" and the text of the Bible.[5] Understanding the way of Christ comes by active discipleship and prayerful reflection. One mark of the Anabaptist hermeneutics that I have been learning is that commitment to the way of Christ in service to the poor and vulnerable is the necessary context for theology. In this regard the insights of Anabaptism and liberation theology come together. The narrative dimension of interpretation, which unleashes the wisdom of contemporary insight from the Spirit who is at work in the world informing and breathing life into the pages of Scripture, has been a potent force in my exegesis. Since my first visit to Brazil, I have discovered a wealth of radical traditions in Christianity—including Anabaptism—where the priority of narrative and biography is acknowledged and the dialectic between present and past, spirit and letter is given its proper place.

Second, in Brazil's CEBs I was struck by ordinary people taking seriously the saying of Jesus that the "babes" understood the ways of God better than the wise and intelligent.[6] I have often recalled my dear friend Alan Kreider pointing me to a passage in the *Martyrs Mirror* that perfectly exemplified so much of what I had experienced in Brazil and that has continued to challenge the interpretative patterns of my lifetime. In Flanders, in the middle of the sixteenth century, a chandler named Jacob was detained for his Anabaptist activities and subsequently questioned by a friar in a local court. During the discussion Jacob quoted the book of Revelation in support of his views, provoking a heated response from his interrogator:

> "What do you understand about St. John's Apocalypse?" the friar asked the chandler. "At what university did you study? At the loom, I suppose? For I understand that you were nothing but a poor weaver and chandler before you went around preaching and rebaptizing. . . . I have attended the university of Louvain, and for long studied divinity, and yet I do not understand anything at all about St. John's Apocalypse. This is a fact." To which Jacob answered: "Therefore Christ thanked his heavenly Father that he had revealed and made it known to babes and hid it from the wise of this world, as it is written in Matt. 11:25." "Exactly!" the friar replied, "God has revealed it

to the weavers at the loom, to the cobblers on the bench, and to bellow-menders, lantern tinkers, scissors grinders, brass makers, thatchers and all sorts of riff-raff, and poor, filthy and lousy beggars. And to us ecclesiastics who have studied from our youth, night and day, God has concealed it."[7]

I used this passage in my inaugural lecture as professor in Oxford[8] as a way of indicating the challenge of the study "from below." At the time of the lecture, however, I did not fully recognize the implications of this for my own scholarship and teaching. Now I can understand better that the "top down" model of theology, which has dominated through the centuries and against which Anabaptists and many others have rightly protested, has to be complemented and, better still, subordinated to a more participative theological enterprise encompassing the Spirit's activity among all God's people. This is stressed in the testimony offered by the early Anabaptists as they appeal to the more participative ethos of 1 Corinthians 14 for their model of ecclesial activity.[9] The opening up of Anabaptist history has reminded us (and we need such reminders on a regular basis) that there is another fascinating side to the Reformation that is not always heard in university courses in theology but that is brim full of vitality and relevance to contemporary debates.[10]

In my theological environment Anabaptism has more negative than positive connotations. To be sure, today there is a more thoroughgoing commitment to a gospel of non-violence and a healthy skepticism of the closeness of the church's relationship to the state. Consequently the contribution of the Anabaptist tradition has offered many a way of conceiving Christian discipleship which rings true to the call of Jesus in the gospels. In one very important respect, however, the idea that one should be an Anabaptist sympathizer leaves people uncomfortable, probably because at the heart of what one is affirming lie misgivings about the mainstream theology of baptism. The nickname Anabaptism rightly suggests sympathy for a more sectarian option and its more costly discipleship. That must be frankly admitted. One consequence has been a tangle of doctrinal and practical predicaments for my wife and me over the years, particularly with regard to the baptism of our own, and others', children.[11]

Taking baptism seriously means needing to recognize and see the best in the "sectarian" inheritance of earliest Christianity, nowhere better exemplified than in the baptismal liturgies of catholic Christianity. I want to affirm and learn from this inheritance as we seek to be faithful to the Christian gospel in an open yet challenging way. The sectarian character of Christian identity is something we all too often quietly ignore, forgetting that emerging Christianity until the time of Constantine was characterized by such a sectarian spirit. The catechumenate was long and thorough, putting to shame our lack of rigor in baptismal preparation.[12] At the heart of the whole baptismal experience is the clear message of a transfer from one dominion to another, involving the acceptance of Jesus Christ as king of kings and lord of lords. The rites of Christian initiation have kept alive that sectarian spirit, which is of the essence of Christianity. What is so striking about the New Testament texts is that they were written by people who had little or no political power. They nevertheless evince a vision of the world at odds with the prevailing ideology, and their writers dared to offer their common life as the pattern for all humanity.[13]

The temptation to self-righteousness is always strong among those influenced by apocalypticism or sectarianism, and it is not difficult to find examples of self-righteousness in the stories of Anabaptist men and women, especially in seeing the church or the world "out there" as in some sense corrupt and contrasting with the pool of light which marks the faithful Christian group. The apocalyptic texts of Judaism and Christianity, which I have spent so much of my working life studying, rarely allow readers the luxury of bathing in certainty. Instead they present a stark challenge to endure, and (particularly in the book of Revelation) to join in the prophetic critique of an unjust and overbearing empire.[14] The New Testament is full of dualistic language, and we may be pardoned for supposing that the first Christians thought that God was present with the community of believers and that the community was therefore in some sense perfect and devoid of sin. Yet the Christian community cannot maintain a superior position with regard to the activity the Spirit of God; the Spirit is not the church's possession, for the church too is under the judgment of God and in need of divine mercy. The coming of the Spirit involves conviction of the world of sin, of justice and judgment. The community of believers, however, does not have a monopoly of righteousness even though their inheritance of the story of God means that they may be best equipped to understand. That is a necessary counterbalance to the sense of superiority and coziness which religious groups can so easily be tempted to cultivate. Part of the wisdom of catholic Christianity has been to foster that sense of suspicion of a church of perfect people this side of the Kingdom of God on earth. Augustine's *City of God* may not be the last word on Christian polity, but it does foster a healthy suspicion of self-righteousness and the propensity of groups to delude themselves. Humility before the mystery of salvation is a fundamental Christian virtue. That humility prized by the Mennonite tradition, is a salutary reminder to all of us about how we should approach our task as theologians in an age where stardom beckons even Christian theologians.

On page after page of the *Martyrs Mirror* one finds stories of brave men and women of the Anabaptist tradition who glimpsed something important in Scripture that made resisting and bearing witness worthwhile. This treasure indicates an approach to theology where narrative and story are central, not some optional extra after reason and argument have taken their place of pre-eminence. Anabaptist theology is different, as Jim McClendon reminds us.[15] It is inclusive, in that it empowers all to share their stories and to learn to find in them signs of God's hand at work. Of course, Anabaptists are not the only ones to understand the importance of such narrative theology. Over the last two decades I have come across scores of people, in historical textbooks and in communities in different parts of the world, doing the same kind of thing. One of the most important things I can do as a Christian theologian is to engage in an act of mediation: to find ways of putting people who are searching for lives of radical discipleship in touch with each other and with their ancestors in the faith. There is something of fundamental importance for the church and the world in the Anabaptist experience of God. It is at the heart of the gospel of Jesus Christ and can, if we attend to it, instruct the world at the start of a new millennium and fructify a theology which is in danger of cutting itself adrift from the understanding that comes from practical discipleship and from those who may best be able to understand and interpret the gospel of Jesus Christ.

CHAPTER EIGHT

Anabaptism as a
Conversation Partner

Stuart Murray

Why did the Anabaptists and the reformers agree that the Bible was authoritative but disagree so profoundly about what the Bible meant and how it applied to their lives and their society? Why did they reach such divergent conclusions, especially about ecclesiology and ethics? What was it about the way they read the same scriptures that produced such very different results—and that prompted the reformers to fear and persecute the Anabaptists?

These were the questions that prompted me to investigate Anabaptist hermeneutics in the late 1980s and subsequently to write a doctoral thesis on the subject.[1] What I discovered was a marginalized approach to biblical interpretation that was radically different from the accepted norms of hermeneutics under Christendom but that had marked similarities to the ways in which several other dissident movements—such as the North African Donatists, French Waldensians and English Lollards—had read the Bible.

This was an approach that was suspicious of the distorting influence of power and status, that empowered ordinary Christians as interpreters, that relied actively on the anticipated guidance of the Holy Spirit, that encouraged congregational hermeneutics and that emphasized application over intellectual discussion. It also took Jesus very seriously and could properly be described as Christocentric rather than Christological: whereas the reformers interpreted the Scriptures with reference to doctrines about the work of Jesus, especially justification by faith, the Anabaptists were interested in Jesus himself, his life and his teaching.

As I studied further and reflected on the implications of this way of reading the Bible, I became increasingly convinced that Anabaptist hermeneutics was not just a topic of historical interest but had contemporary significance. Several of the issues debated by Anabaptists, reformers and spiritualists in the sixteenth century are still unresolved, but the Anabaptist contributions on these issues have rarely received adequate attention. Furthermore, three major shifts in the world church have occurred during the twentieth century, all of which have had important hermeneutical consequences. And on each of these Anabaptist perspectives have something to offer.

First, the steady demise of Christendom in Europe and North America makes it urgent to identify viable post-Christendom alternatives in the areas of theology, missiology, ecclesiology and biblical interpretation. The church has been moved to the margins, and we simply can no longer afford to think or behave as though we were still in the Christendom era. Second, the center of gravity in the church has shifted from the First World to the Third World; most Christians are non-western, non-white, non-wealthy. Different interpretations of the Bible and new ways of reading it have been developing in the Third World, even if many western theologians still regard them as "voices from the margins."[2] Third, the explosive recent growth of Pentecostal and charismatic Christianity poses questions about the adequacy of interpretive practices which marginalize the work of the Holy Spirit and rely heavily on intellectual prowess and academic research.

Anabaptism, I believe, can be a helpful conversation partner with post-Christendom interpreters struggling to operate from the margins rather than the center, with Third World theologians whose principles and perspectives resonate so strongly with the sixteenth-century radicals, and with charismatic Christians searching for a way to hold together Spirit and Word as they reflect both on the Bible and on their own experiences. An approach that was marginalized nearly five centuries ago now seems remarkably relevant in a context where the practices and conclusions of the dominant reformers appear less and less helpful.

But how did I discover the Anabaptists? This tradition has little history in England, nor did I have any family links with it. My roots were in an evangelical Plymouth Brethren church, my school was Anglican, I came to faith through an ex-Methodist church, and I had been deeply impacted by the charismatic movement as a law student in London. After university I moved to Tower Hamlets, one of the poorest and most culturally diverse urban communities in England, where I worked for twelve years as a church planter and cross-cultural missionary. Although the church grew and there were many signs of encouragement in the work, my own evangelical and charismatic heritage did not seem adequate for the challenges I was encountering. I found myself searching for further resources to interpret and respond to the huge and complex issues of poverty, injustice, structural evil, violence and community breakdown that formed the context for my ministry.

From time to time I discovered articles or books that helped me, and I gradually realized that several of these were written by Mennonites. Who were the Mennonites? And why did a tradition that seemed so typically rural have so much to say to an urban church planter on issues of peace, justice, community and lifestyle? Through a mutual friend I met Alan and Eleanor Kreider, missionaries with the Mennonite Board of Mission, and through them I discovered the resources of the London Mennonite Centre. When offered an opportunity to take a break from urban mission and engage in postgraduate research, I chose to explore the Anabaptist tradition from which these Mennonites drew their inspiration.

Studying the Anabaptist movement—and following the radical tradition back through the centuries as I listened for echoes in other dissident movements[3]—I recognized the overwhelming and malign influence of the Constantinian shift on European Christianity—as well as on the world church through the missionary endeavors of European Christians. In books, articles and academic workbooks in the past decade I have attempted to recover various components of this alternative tradition that seem to offer important insights and perspectives for the church in our contemporary post-Christendom context.

For the past eight years I have been involved in theological education and ministerial formation as the director of church planting and evangelism at Spurgeon's College, the largest of the four English Baptist seminaries. In this capacity I have been deeply involved in the British church planting movement. I have visited new churches in many parts of Britain, serving as a trainer, mentor, strategist and consultant, and I have helped to initiate various new church planting ventures.[4] Along the way, two questions have persistently engaged my attention: What is the good news in our society? and What kinds of churches incarnate this good news? I have drawn heavily and gratefully on the Anabaptist tradition as I have wrestled with these questions, discussed them with students and written on evangelism and church planting.[5]

Some missiologists have identified sixteenth-century Anabaptism as a classic example of a missionary movement, where missiology and ecclesiology were not separated as they so often have been throughout church history. In the British context, where churches are emerging from Christendom and recognizing the need to re-invent themselves as missionary congregations, Anabaptism offers an instructive paradigm. In a culture where fewer people know the Christian story but many are looking for a way of living authentically rather than merely a ticket to heaven, the tradition's emphases on the person and life of Jesus and on the call to follow him in life are also helpful and challenging.

I have also written case studies of the distorting influence of the Constantinian shift and the contribution of the Anabaptist tradition. The subject of church discipline, for example, generally provokes very negative reactions among Christians, carrying with it connotations of judgmental attitudes, punishment and the exercise of ecclesiastical power. This is not surprising, given its association in the Christendom era with clericalism, inquisition and coercion. But the radical tradition has insisted that the process described in Matthew 18 and elsewhere in the New Testament is essential for the formation of communities of disciples. Lacking experience and models of good practice, dissenting groups have not always handled this process well (as their critics have frequently pointed out), but Anabaptists and others have at least left a challenging legacy of experimentation with this neglected aspect of local church life. We will need to appropriate and work on this legacy if we are to form the kinds of loving communities that will nurture faithful discipleship in an increasingly alien environment.[6]

One of the most disturbing elements of Anabaptism is the insistence that spirituality and economics belong together. The willingness of Anabaptists to question the sacred notion of private property—whether through the Hutterite community of goods or the Mennonite provision of mutual aid—was deeply threatening to their contemporaries and remains a powerful challenge in our individualistic and consumeristic culture. Reflecting on this, I decided to examine the dominant Christendom tradition of tithing, which some Swiss Anabaptists vehemently opposed and which seems to have so little basis in either the New Testament or the pre-Constantine churches. Tracing the sorry history of tithing between the fourth century and the present day has been salutary—a worrying example of both biblical interpretation subservient to political and economic demands and of the way in which Constantinian reflexes continue to characterize churches in post-Christendom.[7] Rediscovering biblical principles such as jubilee and koinonia—and learning from the

economic practices of the early churches and the radical tradition—is crucial for the formation of churches that will be
good news to the poor and can engage with integrity in holistic mission.

During the past eight years I have also been the editor of
Anabaptism Today, the journal of the Anabaptist Network in
the United Kingdom. This network of Christians from a wide
range of traditions sponsors study groups, runs conferences,
and offers resources from the Anabaptist tradition to those
concerned about radical discipleship in contemporary society. Its growth and influence during the past decade has been
remarkable in a nation devoid of Anabaptist influence for
four centuries. Increasing numbers of Christians have
described their encounter with Anabaptism as "coming
home."[8] In a context where Anabaptism is generally relegated to a dismissive footnote in textbooks, the necessary theological foundation for this network has been provided by the
formation of an Anabaptist Theological Circle, convened by
Alan Kreider, and by the development at Spurgeon's College
of a postgraduate course in Baptist and Anabaptist Studies
(now also offered at the International Baptist Theological
Seminary in Prague and as an open learning course).[9]

Articles in *Anabaptism Today* and other journals have given
me further opportunities to explore aspects of the Anabaptist
tradition and its contemporary significance as a conversation
partner. One aspect of the tradition, which seems to have
received inadequate attention from Mennonite historians, is
the charismatic dimension of some of the sixteenth-century
congregations. Expectation of the Holy Spirit's guidance,
empowering and intervention is apparent from several
Anabaptist documents, and reports of Anabaptist gatherings
suggest that charismatic phenomena were present at the
heart of the movement as well as on its periphery. The
appropriation of this aspect of the movement, though perhaps uncongenial in some circles, may be important if
Anabaptism is to develop a mutually instructive conversation with contemporary charismatic movements.[10]

Another Anabaptist reflex, although not one which seems to have characterized all the early congregations by any means, is what Eleanor Kreider calls "multi-voiced church life." The disempowering of ordinary Christians under Christendom related not only to biblical interpretation but to many other aspects of congregational life—worship, breaking bread, learning together, church discipline, evangelism, pastoral ministry and much else. An early Swiss Brethren tract, explaining why they did not attend the state churches, complained about the monopoly of the preacher and the failure to obey Paul's instructions in 1 Corinthians 14 that every member should contribute when the church met together.[11] One aspect that I have explored, both through writing and in practice, is interactive preaching, in which many voices are heard as church members listen together to the Bible and share their insights.[12]

From September 2000 I will be on sabbatical for a year, and I look forward to the opportunity to continue learning from the Anabaptist tradition, through reading and through interaction with North American Mennonites and neo-Anabaptists in other parts of the world.

I hope to delve more deeply into those aspects of the Anabaptist tradition that I find to be less helpful, or at least less fully developed—according to my current understanding. Thus, as I examined Anabaptist hermeneutics, I valued the determination to listen to Jesus and to not allow Old Testament texts to become pretexts for setting aside New Testament teaching (as the reformers seemed to be doing), but I was not satisfied with the Anabaptists' treatment of the Old Testament.

Another issue has emerged as I have reflected on the popularity of the Celtic tradition among British Christians, prompted partly by a recent conference entitled "There's Life in the Roots" in which members of Celtic and Anabaptist networks shared their perspectives and learned from each other. I have wondered about the relative paucity of Anabaptist resources for personal spirituality, by comparison with the

Celtic tradition, and about the contrast between the world-affirming Celtic tradition and the more world-denying Anabaptist approach. This has caused me to think about ways in which other conversation partners might participate in the adventure of discovering how to follow Jesus in post-Christendom.

But I anticipate that the Anabaptist heritage will continue to function as my primary conversation partner. For I remain deeply suspicious of the pervasive influence of Christendom on my thinking and on the expectations and practices of churches I know, and I am eager to explore other facets of the Anabaptist (and broader dissenting) tradition and its legacy of resistance to Constantinian thinking.

CHAPTER NINE

Meeting the Radical Reformation

Eoin de Bhaldraithe

I was born in the west of Ireland shortly before World War II. We often boasted that there was no Protestant, policeman or public house in our parish. In contemporary language we could say that we were ethnically (or religiously) pure. No doubt many readers of this journal would call us "Constantinian." By the time I had completed second-level schooling at eighteen, I had never met a Protestant socially. We were, however, well versed in the history of the religious wars in Europe. Our education taught us who we were: Irish Catholics oppressed by the Protestants for centuries. Indeed, Ireland is best known worldwide for this Catholic-Protestant divide.

In 1956 I joined the Cistercians or Trappists. The Cistercians are a twelfth-century reform of the Benedictines, while the Trappists are a reform of the Cistercians. Armand de Rancé, the reforming abbot of La Trappe, was the spiritual director of the Catholic James II, who was defeated in Ireland by the Protestant William III in one of the most decisive Catholic-Protestant battles of all time. Thus my decision to join this particular order was unconsciously in line with the sectarian ethos of the time. Nevertheless, my formation as a Christian in the monastery was soon to be influenced by Catholic involvement in ecumenism, one part of which included an encounter with the Radical Reformation.

Lectio Divina

Our monastic training introduced us to the devotional reading of scripture, to which we were to dedicate at least half an hour daily, in addition to hearing the numerous passages read in the liturgy. St. Teresa of Avila once said that all one needs to become contemplative is to say the "Our Father," but one should spend an hour saying it. To which I would add, read the Sermon on the Mount but spend a month reading it; read the Gospel of Matthew but spend a year reading it.

This was the early church tradition of *lectio divina*, or "divine reading," whereby scripture becomes a message from God himself, received in faith and obedience. The Second Vatican Council put it as follows: "Prayer should accompany the reading of sacred scripture, so that a dialogue takes place between God and the reader. . . ." The text continues with a quotation from St. Ambrose: "We speak to him when we pray; we listen to him when we read the divine oracles."[1]

I remember spending a year or more reading St. Matthew's Gospel. The Sermon on the Mount constantly drew me back. I wondered about its pacifism. It was certainly a guide for one's personal life, and there was plenty of opportunity to put it into practice in the close community life we lived. However, as I was being introduced to the general body of Catholic teaching, I was not concerned much about how it would apply to the attitudes of the church itself.

Our theological training tended to reinforce the sectarian mentality. I recall my intense interest in learning of Calvin's view of predestination and how the Jansenists strove to import the doctrine into the Catholic Church under a thin disguise. I was about half way through this course when Pope John called the Second Vatican Council, which was to initiate a Catholic ecumenism. After ordination I was sent to the Benedictine university in Rome where Magnus Löhrer from Einsiedeln, Switzerland, was just beginning to teach dogmatic theology, to which he brought an enthusiastic ecumenical dimension. My training hitherto had been an intensely apologetic introduction to medieval and Counter Reformation theology. Now we were being taught how to read the writings of the early church period. A new mentality was necessary which involved dropping the polemical approach and seeing the Fathers as presenting the message of Christianity in its totality. For a whole year I was at sea until eventually I achieved a turn about which was nothing short of an intellectual conversion, one side effect of which was much new material for "divine reading."

It seemed clear during those years in Rome that I would have great scope for ecumenical activity when I returned to Ireland. When I did come back, the Troubles had not yet begun. Protestant ministers, however, complained continually about the mixed marriage situation, which seemed a worthy cause to study. The promises demanded by the Catholic church that both partners would raise all their children as Catholic were altogether too severe. Although changes were made in the law, they were rather ambiguous and were interpreted in one way on the continent while in English-speaking countries things proceeded as if there had been virtually no change. Many people felt that I was letting down the Catholic side by advocating changes in child-rearing so strongly. Eventually new patterns evolved and now children tend to be brought up in both churches, a practice called "double belonging."

The Irish Conflict

During those years I also watched the painful unfolding of the Irish conflict. It began as a peaceful movement modeled on the civil rights campaign in the U.S. However, there was no tradition of nonviolent protest in Ireland. Gandhi's movement was virtually unknown or was seen only as a parallel to the Irish struggle for freedom, which made it perhaps inevitable that the Irish conflict would very quickly descend into violence. After the initial promise of a nonviolent phase, a terrible tragedy of violence ensued. Advice from the

Catholic clergy seemed to be ineffective. The methods were wrong but the cause was right, the church seemed to say. But saying that the violence was not justified seemed to imply that it could be justified in another situation or even in the judgment of another person. Many Catholics held that, since the IRA were themselves soldiers, their killings were not murder.

At about this time I saw a review of *The Politics of Jesus* by John Howard Yoder in the Jesuit periodical *Theological Studies*.[2] This work of a genuine pacifist was worth buying. I was impressed with the vast number of biblical studies he cited and, moreover, by the valuable new insights Yoder offered into the Christian way of dealing with power and violence. Another book I read at the time was by Stanley Windass who quoted Suarez, the seventeenth-century Jesuit theologian, as saying that it was officially heresy in the Catholic church to espouse a pacifist position.[3] Suarez's theology was "ruthless" and "logical in its philosophy of violence."[4] Yet the teachings of Suarez remained the official Catholic position until the 1970s.

All this time the combined effect of constant reading in the New Testament, my life in the community, and the desperate deeds done by my fellow Catholics in Northern Ireland made me more and more convinced that a disciple of Jesus had to be pacifist. To this emotional preparation, books like Yoder's gave firm intellectual content.

Pope John Paul II

In 1979 the newly elected Pope came to Ireland. In comparison with what the local Catholic bishops were saying, Pope John Paul II took such a strongly pacifist line, that I wrote a long commentary on his speeches.[5] Bishop Cahal Daly, who was later to become leader of the Irish bishops, had published his speeches on the Irish situation in two volumes, which made it easy to compare Daly and the Pope. I found quite a difference! But I also needed to use Yoder's book as a kind of control. How did the Pope compare with this genuine pacifist? Daly seemed to be operating from the old classical position of the just-war theory which was held by all the mainline churches. The Pope had moved well beyond that.

I cannot say that John Paul II had adopted any particular position on the debate between just-war and pacifism. He was profoundly shocked at the Irish violence, especially that of the Catholics, and was simply trying to speak to the situation with words from the gospel. Readers may remember that, in the week before he arrived, Catholic paramilitaries had killed seventeen soldiers in the North and assassinated Lord Mountbatten in the South. In the article I claimed that it was possible to be basically a pacifist but to regard the just-war theory as an "interim ethic," that is, something that may help to limit the violence when the conflict is actually in progress. One passage will explain my attitude at the time which has since become the official Catholic position:

> There seem to be three theological options then. You may take the just war theory as the guiding principle. You may take the pacifist option and regard the other as simply wrong and unworthy. Or you may regard this latter as "interim," as having some value in the actual war situation, but still regarding the ideal of Jesus as normative.

In either of the last two cases you will always be able to preach the gospel to the full. There will never be any need to glorify revolution or war. If you accept the first option, you will be very limited in what you can preach. You will differ from the belligerents only in your assessment of when violence becomes justified. You will never be able to say that violence is the way of hatred because you do believe that it may sometimes be the way of love. The sword-word will be outside your vocabulary. It will not be possible to repeat the patristic preference of being killed to killing. I feel that you will be preaching only half the gospel, or better, only half-preaching the gospel.[6]

When the article was published I sent a copy to Yoder,

who wrote to a newly formed group of Mennonites living in Dublin, advising them to contact me. In the first letter, Dawn Ruth Nelson said they were particularly impressed by my views on "half-preaching the gospel." This led to a most fruitful acquaintance with a historic pacifist church. At one stage I was able to attend their Sunday worship once a year, and our bishop easily gave me permission to preach.

Michael Sattler

Another step in my relationship with the wider Mennonite church was the gift of a copy of a new biography of Michael Sattler.[7] Here was the Radical Reformation which evolved alongside the other Reformation we knew so well in Ireland. In a lengthy review of the book I recorded my excitement at the discovery.[8] A Benedictine, like myself, he left his Black Forest monastery in 1525, was "anabaptized," and produced the Schleitheim confession before he was executed by the Catholics. Nowadays we would all agree that he was a "martyr."

The tenets of Schleitheim that especially tend to impress Catholics include the following:

– People are to be baptized only when they desire to walk in the resurrection and have a mature faith.
– The Christian will not bear the sword of war because Christ did not use.
– Neither will they use the sword of government since Christ did not allow them to make him a king. Catholics tend to regard Romans 13:3-4 as a code of behavior for the good magistrate, whereas Yoder saw it as an exhortation to the Christian to submit to the powers.[9]

It also comes as a surprise that in the Apostolic Tradition and all its variants the magistrate and his sword-bearer are not allowed to come to baptism. Perhaps even more surprising is that this proscription remained in Catholic canon law as an impediment to ordination until 1983! Even Bernard of Clairvaux, theologian of the crusades and of the military orders, said that he was forbidden to wield the sword.[10]

For Sattler, "the commands of scripture" become a "rule of life." This "rule" is to be observed with all the fervor of the "strict observance" that existed in virtually every religious order at the time. Some call this a "monasticized" view of scripture. Trithemius, a Benedictine who wrote just before Sattler's time, said that the two means of monastic renewal were a return to the Rule of Benedict and the direct study of the scriptures. As Catholic reaction to the Reformation developed, Catholics emphasized almost exclusively the observance of the Rule.

Following Vatican II, however, we Catholics were told that "since the final norm of the religious life is the following of Christ as it is put before us in the gospel, this must be taken by all institutes as the supreme rule."[11] Let us hope that we do not do this in a Jewish sense. Whatever good works we do, God has created them for us to walk in them. Chapter 4 of the Rule of Benedict gives a list of "instruments of good works." The list is actually an earlier rule made for Christians in general and is closely related to the Irish monastic rules that survive.[12] It also reminds us of the third chapter of the Letter of Cyprian to Quirinius.[13]

From the Radical Reformation, then, we have much to learn about Christ's teaching on peace. However we deal with war when it occurs, we have no escape from the binding force of the words of Jesus. In him we achieve victory over violence and not through violence. The practice of adult baptism produces a community of true believers with great potential for excluding the nominal Christian. However, I find it difficult to accept that those baptized in infancy do not include true Christians. Catholics view the Eucharist as a meal of union celebrated by those who are already the body of Christ.

Anabaptism

While the Anabaptists have very clear views on what one must do to be a Christian, it must be disconcerting at times to meet a person with a very deep Christian spirit who has not followed the rules. When I had just returned from Rome a member of the Church of Christ tried to convince me that I needed to be "anabaptized" if I were to be an authentic Christian. I withstood his conclusions, but his arguments did have a profound effect on me. Some people are deeply devoted to Christ even though they have not followed the rules that I consider essential, for myself at least. Pope Pius XII had insisted that the Roman Catholic church alone is the Body of Christ. The Second Vatican Council felt obliged to change this and say that "church" is also found outside our church. So just as some Anabaptists would not regard me as a proper Christian, my church also has difficulty in accepting them as fully belonging to the Body of Christ.

Perhaps the most worrying feature of my contact with Protestants is the evangelical attitude, which is especially true of those who have remained more faithful to the original reforming vision. They have retained so much of the early fervor that they are strongly anti-Catholic. We Catholics think that we have changed greatly in the last forty years and so should be the object of a more benign judgment. All this suggests that there is still plenty of scope for ecumenical activity. Repentance and forgiveness are needed on all sides.

Joseph Liechty insists that our repentance must have a corporate dimension, which he argues is very important in Ireland. For if there is to be any just and lasting peace, we must deal with the legacy of sectarianism. I am happy to record that Liechty, a member of the original Mennonite community in Dublin, is one of the most effective preachers of repentance to us Irish. As an outsider he is in the unique position of being able to speak impartially to both Catholics and Protestants.[14] Because of the corporate nature of the process, those with least guilt can be foremost in repenting on behalf of the community. Some months after Liechty's article on repentence was published, Archbishop Carey of Canterbury, preaching in Dublin, asked forgiveness for "our often brutal domination" of the Irish. A few months later Cardinal Daly, preaching in Canterbury, asked forgiveness for the many wrongs inflicted on the British, especially during the last twenty-five years of conflict. More important, because it was more appreciated by the Protestant side, Bishop William Walsh apologized for the pain and hurt caused by the mixed marriage laws.[15]

The theme of repentance has now become more universal. Recently in a ceremony on the first Sunday of Lent, the Pope asked forgiveness for Catholic sins. A corresponding document was published by the Vatican's International Theological Commission. Though extremely cautious, it does contain the following statement:

In the period from the close of the (Second Vatican) Council until today resistance to its message has certainly saddened the Spirit of God (cf. Eph. 4:30). To the extent that some Catholics are pleased to remain bound to the separations of the past, doing nothing to remove the obstacles that impede unity, one could justly speak of solidarity in the sin of division (cf. 1 Cor. 1:10-16). In this context the words of the Decree on Ecumenism could be recalled: "With humble prayer we ask pardon of God and of the separated brethren, as we forgive those who trespass against us."[16]

Since the denominations were born and grew apart in mutual recrimination, the way back seems to be self incrimination before God.

Conversations

When I visited the Associated Mennonite Biblical Seminary in Elkhart in 1985, I found very little interest in dialogue with Catholics. But since then official conversations have been launched, and John A. Rodano has described the two meetings that have taken place.[17] Like me, he was surprised by the distinction between the classical and Radical Reformations. The radicals tend to speak of the "Constantinian fall." "Catholics," he says, "insist on the continuity of the apostolic church through every different historical period. . . ." After all the apologies from Catholic leaders, perhaps this statement should be a little less assertive. Rodano tells us that members of the dialogue group have different views on the status of infants, which points to the need for a more profound study of the theology of baptism.

Indeed, I see a unique opportunity in these conversations to produce statements on baptism and pacifism. In 1983 the Anglican-Roman Catholic International Commission was asked to produce a document on grace and salvation. On the advice of Henry Chadwick and others, the commission decided they would not study the question independently but simply adopt the main conclusions of the Lutheran-Catholic dialogue on the same issue. Because the issues of adult baptism and pacifism have not been the subject of joint study so far, they offer a unique opportunity for discussion by this group. The main Catholic contribution to such a discussion might be as follows.

Baptism

We Catholics have produced a new rite of initiation of adults,[18] involving baptism, anointing and eucharist. Very much admired and imitated by other churches, this rite is to be used even for children as young as seven or eight who wish to become Catholics, even though "ordinary" children will not receive the anointing until some years later. From the Mennonite point of view, however, we still baptize infants. Yet our church insists today that children must not be baptized unless there is a solid hope that they will be reared as Christians.[19] Thus we have outlawed indiscriminate baptism. Though it may still be practiced in some places, it is not now church policy. Many parents believe that children should not be baptized since in early adulthood they will encounter an agnostic attitude on the university campus. They should at that stage be allowed to make up their own minds. Whether or not baptism is conferred depends again on the attitude of the parents. Such developments narrow the gap between the traditional paedobaptists and Anabaptists.

Regarding the history of baptism, an instruction by the

Vatican some years ago argued that both adult and infant baptism were acceptable in the early church. Although the Apostolic Tradition was cited as a witness to baptizing infants, scholars nowadays rely somewhat less on this kind of statement, especially as other parts of the document presume a more mature individual. So too, the document cites the witness of early inscriptions, without admitting that they might be referring only to emergency baptism when the infant was in danger of death.[20] Evidently there is ample opportunity for learning together from those who have walked before us in the way of faith.

Peace

Thank God pacifism is no longer a Catholic heresy. The change is due mainly to the influence of Thomas Merton,[21] son of a Quaker mother whose views exercised a strong influence on him. But his reading of Roland Bainton eventually convinced him that the Catholic church was ill-advised to follow Augustine.[22] Merton's thought and especially his opposition to the Vietnam war occasioned the Pastoral Letter of the U.S. bishops.[23] Despite all the space this document gives to the just-war theory, it has also won the freedom for Catholics to hold a pacifist view.

In Vienna in 1983, on the third centenary of the defeat of the Turks, Pope John Paul II said:

> We understand that *the language of arms is not the language of Jesus Christ* . . . armed combat is, at best, an inevitable ill in which even Christians may be . . . involved. . . . [Christ] turns every one of my enemies into a brother of mine, a brother who is worthy of my love even as I defend myself against his onslaught.[24]

Here war is "at best, an inevitable ill." The right of self-defense is upheld, however, in terms very close to Augustine.

Early in 1991 when the Gulf War erupted, the Pope advised the United States against it. Afterwards an article appeared with the Pope as its main author.[25] The following summary seems to indicate the official Catholic position on warfare at the moment: Past views on war are inadequate since modern warfare has become so lethal. There follows a historical section, beginning with the pacifism of Origen and the Apostolic Tradition. Then a profound change took place under Constantine and Theodosius, for whom war became a sad necessity. In the Middle Ages the church declared herself against war. The crusades, however, were just and meritorious. The wars of religion (1520-1700) involved the Catholic church on one side. It was only in this century (about 1915) that popes became totally opposed to war. The just-war theory is then described with the claim that it was never "official" Catholic teaching. Its purpose was to limit warfare. But in fact the conditions required were unattainable. The theory should be abandoned. War is not only immoral but unreasonable. The church must preach the gospel and insist that "those who construct peace" are blessed because they are children of God. The church therefore condemns war and promotes peace.

That this is not exactly a pacifist view is clear in how the Constantinian mutation is justified. Yet there has been considerable movement toward pacifism on the part of the Catholic church. To engage in dialogue with pacifists on this matter would be of great advantage in clarifying our positions further.

Conclusion

Like the Quakers, the Mennonites and Hutterites have exerted an influence far beyond their numbers. Here I have described the effect they have had on my own Christian development. Now my church is in official dialogue with them. Let us hope that this encounter might change the Catholic church and draw it closer to Christ himself.

CHAPTER TEN

Reflections on My Encounter with the Anabaptist-Mennonite Tradition

Richard J. Mouw

Herman Hoeksema was a brilliant Christian Reformed pastor-theologian who in the 1920s criticized the teaching, long held by Calvinists, that in addition to the saving grace that God bestows only on the elect, there is a "common grace," an attitude of divine favor that results in certain benefits for the human race as a whole. In 1924 Hoeksema and his followers were forced out of the Christian Reformed Church, and they established their own denomination, the Protestant Reformed Church. When Hoeksema later reflected on the controversy of the 1920s, he wrote with special bitterness about the way his theological perspective had been characterized by the Christian Reformed leadership: "And all that opposed them and refused to believe and proclaim this theory of common grace, they proudly and disdainfully branded as Anabaptist!"[1]

The rhetoric directed against Hoeksema by his theological opponents has been a common tactic in the Calvinist tradition. When the going gets really tough in an intra-Reformed controversy, one of the parties will frequently reach into the rhetorical arsenal and employ what seems to be one of the worst insults one Calvinist can toss at another: "Anabaptist!"

Reformed thinkers have been all too eager to portray Anabaptist thought as dangerous and unworthy of serious theological engagement. The best known example of this habit is Article 36 of the 1561 Belgic Confession, where the Reformed churches make it clear that they "detest the Anabaptists and other seditious people" for the way in which they "reject the higher powers and magistrates, and would subvert justice, introduce a community of goods, and confound that decency and good order which God hath established among men."[2]

I have devoted quite a bit of my energy during my scholarly career in attempting both to understand this hostility and to do my part to counteract it within the Reformed community.

Encounters

My interest in Reformed-Anabaptist relations grew out of very practical patterns of social involvement. My graduate study on secular university campuses occurred in the 1960s. Having been sensitized to issues of justice and peace by the witness of the civil rights movement, I became convinced that the United States' military involvement in Southeast Asia was seriously misguided, and I actively protested those policies. This kind of political involvement did not fit well the dominant mood of the evangelicalism of that time. But in the early 1970s it became clear that many of us had been engaged in a lonely effort to reconcile evangelical convictions with an activist spirit. We found each other, and a new kind of evangelical witness was expressed through the 1973 Chicago Declaration of Evangelical Social Concerns, magazines like *The Other Side* and *The Post-American*, and the Evangelicals for Social Action organization.

My own impulse was to undergird this new evangelical activism with careful theological reflection. Joining the philosophy faculty at Calvin College provided me with an excellent opportunity to explore the Reformed tradition, and I found many riches there. Obviously John Calvin's own significant involvement in political life provided an important model, but I was especially intrigued by the life and thought of Abraham Kuyper, who loomed so large as a public leader in the Netherlands in the last half of the 19th century: among other accomplishments, Kuyper founded a political party, which he in turn led as a member of the Dutch parliament, and he even served for a few years as prime minister.

When Kuyper delivered the Stone Lectures at Princeton Seminary in 1898, he went out of his way to offer a rather harsh critique of the Anabaptist perspective, specifically rejecting the Anabaptist insistence that the earthly ministry of Jesus provides us with an ethical model according to which we are to distance ourselves from accepted patterns of citizenship. This wrongly presumes, insisted Kuyper, that Jesus came to replace the Old Testament standards for righteous politics with a new set of ethical requirements. Kuyper vigorously rejected the argument that the earthly ministry of Jesus introduces new moral-political content. Jesus was no innovator in this regard, said Kuyper. "Can we imagine that at one time God willed to rule things in a certain moral order, but that now, in Christ, He wills to rule it otherwise?" he asked. "Verily Christ has swept away the dust with which man's sinful limitations had covered up this world-order, and has made it glitter again in its original brilliancy."[3]

At about the time when I was exploring these themes in Kuyper's thought, I also read John Howard Yoder's *The Politics of Jesus*. While I was not convinced by all that Yoder argued for in developing his *imitatio Christi* perspective for a contemporary social ethic, I was intrigued by the overall case that he made, and I was definitely convinced that Yoder's version of the Anabaptist ethic could not be dismissed as easily as Kuyper and other Reformed thinkers seemed to assume. I tried to explore these matters carefully in my writings, especially in my 1976 book, *Politics and the Biblical*

Drama,[4] where I called for a new Reformed-Anabaptist dialogue and offered some thoughts—friendly ones, I thought—about where I both agreed and disagreed with John Yoder's position.

Much to my surprise, Yoder was not amused. He sent me a copy of a privately circulated response to my book, in which he argued that I seriously misunderstood him at a number of key points. He also expressed to me his displeasure at the fact that I had chosen to spend so many pages directly discussing his views. He counseled me that I would do better to develop my own positive perspective, rather than to engage in what he saw as a negative critique of his writings.

Fortunately, many others in the Anabaptist academic community came to a different assessment of my efforts. They rightly saw that my primary intention was not to "refute" Yoder, or to seek to make my fortune by being known as his most persistent opponent, but rather to initiate from the Calvinist side a new and more productive kind of Anabaptist-Reformed dialogue. Consequently, I was invited to make the rounds of Mennonite campuses, giving lectures and engaging in dialogue. In the years immediately following the publication of my book I visited Bluffton, Goshen, Elkhart, Hillsboro, and North Newton. Not only did these travels give me a wonderful opportunity for discussions with Anabaptist scholars in a variety of academic disciplines, but I also received a few lessons in playing the Mennonite Game!

One stimulating event in that period was a symposium in Kansas City, where scholars representing a range of expertise offered their critiques of *The Politics of Jesus.* I was one of the few non-Anabaptists invited to attend, and John Yoder seemed to accept my critical probings with more appreciation than he had previously.

Later on Yoder and I joined forces from both sides of the Reformed-Anabaptist divide to argue that the disputes between Calvinists and Anabaptists are not based on disagreements between radically different theological types.

Rather, they are elements in intra-family argument. These disputes reach a high intensity because the differences between the two groups are of a more intimate character than are the arguments of either group with, say, the Lutherans or the Catholics.[5]

I was helped in coming to this assessment by two sources within the Reformed community. One was the Dutch scholar Willem Balke's careful study of the sixteenth-century setting.[6] Balke showed that John Calvin's own frustrations with the Anabaptists had to do with the fact that the Anabaptists "out-Calvinisted" the Reformed community on at least two important points. The first was church discipline. The Calvinists were very critical of Catholics and Lutherans for their lack of attention to the role of discipline in the Christian community. The Anabaptists, however, took discipline even further than the Calvinists, insisting on very tight patterns of communal control. The Calvinists, obviously stung by this criticism, responded by labeling the Anabaptists as "perfectionist."

The second point had to do with church-world relations. Calvinism has been well known for its stark portrayal of human depravity. But Reformed thinkers, having started with this strong emphasis on human sinfulness, regularly introduced modifications—of the sort associated with "common grace" teachings attacked by Herman Hoeksema—that allowed them to endorse some of the things going on in the larger culture, especially the workings of civil government. On this point too the Anabaptists chided them for their inconsistency, insisting that a negative assessment of unregenerate human nature required a strict posture of separation from the world. Here the Calvinist response featured the kind of condemnatory language that showed up in the article from the Belgic Confession, mentioned above.

The other source that helped me much were the writings of Leonard Verduin, a Christian Reformed pastor whose affection for the Anabaptists is well known in the Mennonite community. He convinced me that it does no good for Reformed people to set important questions aside by accusing people within the Reformed community of being closet Anabaptists because they manifest "perfectionism" and "spiritual arrogance." Verduin pointed out, for example, that the "believers' church" emphasis of the Anabaptists resurfaces within the "experiential" strain of Dutch Calvinism: Mennonites will only baptize people who have had an experience of conversion; experiential Calvinists will only baptize the children of *parents* who have had an experience of conversion.[7] Along similar lines, the strong preference of Dutch Calvinist pietists for a "gathered" church versus a "territorial" church[8] parallels an important feature of Anabaptist ecclesiology.

All of this is of more than taxonomical interest for me. I have not simply been interested in the ways in which the standard debates between Reformed and Anabaptist thinkers should be seen as occurring within the same theological family. I have also been forced by these considerations to look with much sympathy at those Anabaptist-type tendencies within the Reformed perspective. And even where I still make some of the tendency-checking moves that are typical of traditional Reformed thought, I have tried to do so with more self-awareness than I often see on these matters in the Reformed tradition. In short, I have tried to be a Calvinist who is not influenced by the pathology that I have labeled "Mennophobia."

Continuing Concerns

I must confess, though, that I have also had to fight other more subtle patterns of thought in my efforts to be more open than many in the Reformed tradition to Anabaptist theology. A special danger has been a kind of condescending fondness for Anabaptist views. It is easy for us outsiders merely to allow ourselves to be "challenged" by the Anabaptists, to see the Radical Reformation as providing a helpful "corrective" to tendencies within our own communities. In thus depicting Anabaptist thought as not constituting a theological system in its own right, we find it easy to continue to marginalize the

Anabaptist perspective by allowing it to function in our minds primarily as providing compensatory emphases whose main value is that they modify other theological schemes.

But this danger is not only in the eye of the outside beholder. During my early tours in the Anabaptist academy I often felt frustrated by a kind of "discipline gap." My own interests were shaped in good part by interests in systematic philosophical thought. But the disciplines that encouraged those patterns did not seem to be held in high esteem on Mennonite campuses, where theological issues were usually addressed mainly by people whose training was in the historical and biblical fields of study. That is not a bad thing as such. I have learned much by being forced to square my systematic interests with the specifics of church history and biblical exegesis. My understanding of Anabaptist life and thought has been greatly enriched by having to wrestle, for example, with the history of the persecution of Anabaptists by "Constantinian" Protestants, as well as with the actual content of the Sermon on the Mount—a biblical text that we Reformed types do not like to have to look at too closely!

However, the overall systematic questions are also important to discuss. One key issue that needs much attention, as I see things, is the question of continuities. We Reformed Christians are much fonder of continuities and fulfillments than we are of disruptions and novelties, whereas the Anabaptists have always seemed eager to emphasize discontinuities—between the Old and New Testaments, for example, as well as in insisting on a radical Protestant break with the "Constantinian" past at the time of the Reformation. These are matters about which Calvinists and Anabaptists need to continue talking. And now that there is a new generation of Mennonite thinkers who have received the highest level of training in philosophy and dogmatics, this kind of discussion can take on a new life in our own day.

There are also some more specific topics that we need to explore more carefully than we have in the past. I worry a bit, for example, about the ways some Mennonites treat such matters as Christology and the atonement. The view of the work of the Cross that John Howard Yoder set forth in *The Politics of Jesus* is a continuing matter of concern for me. When a strong emphasis is placed on imitating the suffering of Christ—as in Yoder's development of the ethical implications of Christ's encounter with "the principalities and powers"—attention is easily diverted away from what classical theology has seen as the *inimitable* features of the work of the Cross, as in Christ the Lamb offering himself as the once-and-for-all substitionary sacrifice on behalf of sinners. I know that Anabaptists have difficulties with the juridical-penal categories that many of us insist upon employing in explicating these dimensions. But I do worry that Anabaptists' skittishness about such matters nudges them a little too far at times in the direction of a liberal-type moralizing about what happened at Calvary.

Even so, my own understanding of Jesus' redemptive mission has been greatly enriched by my encounter with Anabaptist thought. I have come to see that Calvinists need to pay more sustained attention to the newness that Jesus was sent to model and accomplish. And I am grateful that we Calvinists can join Anabaptists and many other Christians today in exploring together what the cost of discipleship means for our present context. As a recovering Mennophobe, my debt to the sons and daughters of the Radical Reformation is immense!

CHAPTER ELEVEN

Embodying the Gospel in Community

Richard B. Hays

One thing I have learned from the Radical Reformers is that theological thought can never be separated from its embodiment in concrete communities of worship and service. Thus, when asked how my thought has been shaped by engagement with Radical Reformation theology, I must reply—in the spirit of what I have learned from the Anabaptist tradition—that I cannot answer the question without explaining how my *life* has been shaped by encounter with radical reformation *communities*.

The Pilgrimage to Community

In the summer of 1971, I decided to drop out of seminary. My one year of study at the Perkins School of Theology at Southern Methodist University had been a disillusioning experience. The United Methodist Church, the church in which I had grown up, seemed to be a vast, cumbersome bureaucracy; my classmates in seminary seemed less concerned about preaching the gospel than about pursuing professional advancement in the denominational pecking order. At least, that was my uncharitable assessment of the situation. My wife Judy and I, newly married, had read Dietrich Bonhoeffer's *The Cost of Discipleship* together and found it compelling but distant from the actual life of the church we had experienced. We had failed to find a congregation in Dallas where we felt nurtured and challenged to grow as disciples of Jesus. I was not sure that ordained ministry was the right vocation for me, and I needed a break to reassess what I was doing. Thus, when an opportunity came for me to teach high school English in Longmeadow, Massachusetts, I seized it.

In Massachusetts we met some people who were interested in starting a Christian intentional community. We had no clear blueprint for what we were doing, but we knew that we wanted a more intense experience of Christian community than we had found in our various denominational churches. Six of us moved into a large old house in Springfield, which we christened The Ark. We developed a pattern of eating meals together, praying together daily, and sharing common expenses. We all read Bonhoeffer's little classic *Life Together* and tried to put into practice his counsel about the practices of confession, forgiveness and mutual accountability. Our Sunday evening Bible study began to attract friends and neighbors, growing into an informal prayer-and-praise fellowship that regularly brought about fifty people together for singing, prayer, Bible study and a potluck supper.

Some of the participants in this larger fellowship were also interested in exploring life in community. Consequently, we began to look around for guidance. We knew about Clarence Jordan's Koinonia Farm community and Francis Schaeffer's L'Abri in Switzerland, but neither of these seemed quite the right model for a house-church community in an urban setting.

In time, we learned about Reba Place Fellowship, a large and well established extended-household community in Evanston, Illinois.[1] Reba Place was the hub for a network of similar communities, most of which had grown from Mennonite roots. We began to draw on their wisdom and experience as our little house-church community slowly took shape. Reba Place sent a delegation of elders to visit us and give counsel, and I, along with several other members of our group, traveled to Evanston to see their community in action.

It was my first encounter with Radical Reformation theology embodied in the flesh. I was moved not only by the community's depth of commitment (in contrast to the tepid mainline Protestant congregations I had known) but also by the gracious beauty and simplicity of their common life, the unassuming maturity and holiness of their long-time members, their candor in confronting sin and failure in the community, and their sustained commitment to hands-on service in their needy, racially mixed neighborhood. I was seeing before my eyes a church that seemed to stand in recognizable continuity with the communities that I had read about in Paul's letters, in Acts 2:42-47 and 4:32-35, and in Bonhoeffer.

In 1974 our community in Massachusetts formally organized itself as Metanoia Fellowship, and the residential community grew from the original one household to four, now encompassing more than thirty adult members along with about fifteen children. We did not think of ourselves as Anabaptists—our members being Episcopalians, Congregationalists, Evangelical Covenanters, Methodists and so forth—but the Anabaptist vision of life in community provided the inspiration for our efforts to lead simple lives of radical discipleship.

The Impact of Yoder's *The Politics of Jesus*

Recognized as one of the pastoral leaders of Metanoia, I soon realized my need for more theological education and began commuting to Yale Divinity School on a part-time basis to continue work on my M.Div. degree. During my studies there I first read John Howard Yoder's *The Politics of Jesus*, which grasped my imagination forcefully.[2] Because I was living in a countercultural community seeking to embody the gospel, I found Yoder's critique of mainline Protestant ethics and his constructive proposals about Jesus as the norm for ethics to be enormously helpful in my own effort to understand and commend the practices of discipleship that my community was seeking to follow.

Yoder's ideas have become so much a part of my own theological framework that it is not easy now to recall precisely all the ways in which *The Politics of Jesus* impacted my thinking twenty-five years ago. At least the following five factors were significant.

1. Yoder provided a clear diagnosis of what I had found unsettling about my theological education. He pinpointed the compromises that made so much Protestant theology appear to be an exercise in apologetics for the status quo: theological ethics in the Niebuhrian tradition rendered Jesus and the gospels mute and irrelevant and thus left the church free to conform itself to the political and economic conventions of its surrounding environment. Once the diagnosis was made, the remedy was clear: the church should be directly guided by the teaching and example of Jesus, not by prudentially calculated approximations of the ideals of love and justice. I began to see that this perspective implied a fundamental critique not only of the mainline establishment church but also of the left-wing politics that had shaped my thinking during my undergraduate years.

2. At the same time that I read Yoder, I was also absorbing Karl Barth's *Church Dogmatics* and the thought of Hans Frei, who championed the recovery of biblical narrative as the proper framework for theology. The conjunction of Yoder with Barth and Frei provided a stimulating matrix for reflection. I wondered whether Yoder's reading of the New Testament demanded a historical reconstruction of the Jesus behind the gospel portraits, or whether his ethical position would have been stronger if he had insisted, with Frei, that the identity of Jesus Christ is disclosed only in the canonical narratives. I also wondered, on the other hand, whether the narratively shaped "Yale theology" I was learning would have more impact and integrity if it were linked with the Anabaptist insistence on discipleship in community. In either case, it was clear to me that Barth and Yoder were prophetic voices who summoned the church to a fresh encounter with the Word of God—a word not of our own devising—that judges us and calls us to be transformed.

3. In reading Yoder, I saw that the modern dichotomy between religion and politics made no sense—or, rather, that it made sense only within the logic of an order inimical to the gospel. I began to grasp more fully that Jesus was not a figure who preached religious ideas that might or might not have political implications; rather, he called followers to a way of life that necessarily entailed the formation of a new *polis.* The kingdom of God was not merely a figure of speech; it was a claim about the concrete manifestation of divine sovereignty in the world. This insight has contributed to my longstanding concern to demonstrate in my work that theology and ethics can never be separated and that we cannot treat issues of discipleship as secondary implications of a more primary set of theological convictions.

4. In particular, I found my attention riveted by Yoder's discussion of Paul's message of justification by grace through faith. Yoder contended that Paul understood justification as "a social phenomenon centering in the reconciliation of different kinds of people."[3] At this point, Yoder was dependent on the work of several New Testament scholars (especially Krister Stendahl, Markus Barth, Hans Werner Bartsch and Paul Minear), but it was through Yoder that I first encountered this interpretation of Paul and saw it placed into a larger construal of the New Testament's message. This tremendously exciting discovery revolutionized my reading of Paul's letters, and it held the potential of overcoming traditional dichotomies between Paul and Jesus. My subsequent work on Paul has sought, in several ways, to develop insights that were first elicited by my reading of Yoder.[4]

5. Finally, I was fascinated by the way Yoder's exposition of the politics of Jesus produced a persuasive construal of the unity of the New Testament's message, a vision of the wholeness of the New Testament canon. The problem of unity and diversity in the canon is a notorious difficulty in biblical scholarship. Yoder's straightforward and forceful reading pulled the diverse voices in the New Testament together into a chorus praising the Lamb who was slain and commending

his life as a pattern for ours. Books as disparate as Luke, Romans, Ephesians and Revelation could be heard, under Yoder's direction, as complementary voices. Yoder pointed the way forward toward a solution of the problem of unity and diversity in New Testament theology.

Readers acquainted with my body of scholarly work will see how these insights, originally derived from Yoder, have been woven through my thought and writing. I reemphasize, however, that my reading of Yoder did not occur in a vacuum. I found his account of Jesus' politics compelling because it corresponded to what I was learning about the Christian life by living in a community also shaped by the witness of the Radical Reformation. Apart from that concrete experience of community life, I doubt that Yoder's themes would have found such resonance in my own emergent theological consciousness.

Dangers and Temptations

At the same time, however, my theological studies also began to uncover for me some of the limitations of the Radical Reformation tradition. As I studied the history of the Reformation, it had seemed to me—as it did to the sixteenth-century Anabaptists—that Luther and Calvin, in their continued defense of infant baptism, were strangely inconsistent with the logic of justification by faith. If we are justified by faith, I asked Professor George Lindbeck, does it not follow that only believers should be baptized? Rather than answering my question, he suggested that I write a paper on the problem. And so, in the last year of my M.Div. studies, I wrote a lengthy paper on "The Relation of Baptism and Justification in the Theology of Luther, Calvin, and the Anabaptists." The driving heuristic question of the paper was: "Is the practice of infant baptism compatible with a consistent adherence to the principle of justification *sola fide*?" I read not only the magisterial reformers but also Conrad Grebel, Balthasar Hubmaier, Menno Simons and the major confessions of the Anabaptist tradition.[5]

As I worked through these writings, I was impressed by

the clarity and courage of the early Anabaptists, and I was persuaded that their understanding of baptism did in fact recover important aspects of the New Testament's teaching. At the same time, however, I was given pause in some cases by what appeared to be flat-footed literalism and hermeneutical naïvete. For example, Grebel's argument against singing in the church: "Whatever we are not taught by clear passages or examples must be regarded as forbidden, just as if it were written: 'This do not: sing not.'. . . We must not follow our notions; we must add nothing to the word and take nothing from it."[6] Alongside this sort of unimaginative rigidity, I was also disturbed by the tendency of many Anabaptist writers to bifurcate reality, juxtaposing the inward and spiritual realm of faith to the outward and physical realm of sacramental action, deprecating the latter in favor of the former. Some Anabaptists regarded baptism not as a divine act of grace but as a human pledge or testimony of faith. Against this tendency, the sturdy sacramental realism of Luther looked highly appealing because it protected the priority of God's gracious action *pro nobis*. Indeed, I came to see that for Luther infant baptism was necessary to safeguard *sola fide* because it so clearly symbolizes that we do *not* determine our salvation by our own decision. The danger of the Anabaptist position is that it can turn faith into a work, a precondition that must be met to receive the grace of God. As Luther warned, here lurks a *Werkteufel* (i.e., a devil that tempts us to rely on works) that evacuates the grace of God and drives us back to constant scrutiny of our own subjective faith experience as the ground of salvation. I remained (and still remain) convinced that the baptism of confessing believers is the practice that most faithfully reflects the New Testament's interpretation of baptism's significance, but I found that Calvin's exposition of baptism as a *covenant* offered a more profound theological framework for understanding baptism than anything I had found in the Anabaptist writers.

Correlated with the danger of turning faith into a work is the tendency of some Anabaptist theology towards a naively optimistic anthropology that assumes a simple and unprob-lematical capacity of human beings to hear and obey God's commandments, an impulse paralleled, of course, by similar tendencies in my own Wesleyan tradition. Here again, I found Luther's theology to be a necessary counterpoint, reminding us of the dark complexity of our own motives and the weakness and limitations of our obedience.

This last theme was of particular relevance for me as I reflected on my own experience of community in Metanoia Fellowship (which ultimately failed and dissolved in the late 1970s). In our worst moments, we were pretty proud of our-selves for being radical Christians ("Lord, we have left every-thing and followed you"), and we were constantly tempted to be judgmental toward outsiders and harshly perfectionis-tic in our dealings with one another within the community. Of course, as we got to know one another better over the years, the reality of our own human sinfulness and broken-ness impressed itself upon us unmistakably. The challenge for us, as for all Christian communities, was to keep the gospel of unmerited grace and the radical imperative of the transformed life in a faithful balance. In that respect, our lit-tle community was recapitulating the struggle that the churches of the sixteenth century had faced.

Key Insights and Unresolved Questions

I am profoundly indebted to Radical Reformation theolo-gy and to the communities that have embodied it. Whatever failings and weaknesses these communities may have had, they have been for me a city set on a hill, a sign of God's com-ing kingdom. As I have sought to discern and write about the New Testament's moral vision,[7] I have been repeatedly instructed and inspired by the testimony of the Radical Reformation tradition. Although it has been more than twen-ty years since my wife and I lived in community, I have been permanently shaped by that experience, and I continue to ponder its theological implications. What are the key themes and insights that have been most important in my own thinking? By way of brief summary, I highlight four points.

1. *The radical call to discipleship.* The Radical Reformation tradition emphasizes that authentic faith is necessarily embodied in a life of following the teaching and example of Jesus. The point seems so simple and fundamental that it should hardly require emphasis, but the history of the church shows our urgent need to be reminded of this truth again and again. Christian theology has constructed numerous rationalizations and evasions, but the Anabaptists—alongside other communities such as the Franciscans—remind us that those who are called to be Jesus' disciples must take up the cross and follow him.

2. *The centrality of life in community.* Our life of discipleship is not a lonely, individualistic project. To be called to follow Jesus is to be called into community. The Radical Reformation tradition wonderfully exemplifies this truth, which must shape our understanding of all Christian doctrines and practices. For example, baptism is not merely a rite conferring forgiveness of sins; rather, it is an incorporation into the eschatological community of God's people. In Anabaptist tradition, the Body of Christ is not only a theoretical doctrine; it is the daily experienced context of life together in a community of mutual love and accountability. The Anabaptist emphasis on mutual admonition and church discipline is deeply faithful to the New Testament picture of the church, and it is an emphasis that the wider Christian church desperately needs to recover if we are to survive and bear witness with integrity in the post-Christendom situation. The rest of the church is only now starting to realize the truth to which the Radical Reformation communities have patiently witnessed for more than four hundred years: the *ekklesia* is a peculiar people, called out of the world to embody a different politics.

3. *Sharing possessions.* That different politics is most dramatically expressed in the Radical Reformation's practices of economic sharing and simple living. Never has this message been more urgently needed than the present. In a world driv-

en by corporate capitalism and drugged into materialistic numbness by the suggestive power of the mass media, the counter-testimony of the Anabaptist communities is crucial for modeling another way, the way of the gospel.

4. *Peacefulness and peacemaking.* Similarly, the Radical Reformation's renunciation of violence is of enormous importance for our time. The church's longstanding complicity with violence is one of the most shameful aspects of its history. By recalling the community of faith to the peaceable teaching and example of Jesus, the Anabaptist tradition summons us to reclaim our true vocation in the world as a sign of the coming kingdom in which, under the lordship of Jesus, "They shall not hurt or destroy on all my holy mountain, for the earth will be full of the knowledge of the Lord as the waters cover the sea" (Is. 11:9).

Reservations and Afterthoughts

To give a full picture of my response to the Radical Reformation tradition, I must balance these appreciative remarks with a few additional critical observations and questions. I have already noted the concerns I had back in the 1970s about the tradition's tendency towards excessive biblical literalism and towards an over-optimistic anthropology that, at its worst, can lead to a semi-Pelagian soteriology and its correlate, a prideful disdain toward outsiders. The recurrent, unimaginative criticism of the Anabaptist tradition as "sectarian" finds its one legitimate target at this point. As I have continued to reflect on the theological implications of the Anabaptist legacy, two other issues have come into focus for me—issues that I believe to be important for the ongoing dialogue between Radical Reformation and mainline Protestant traditions.

First, how do we take adequate account theologically of the Old Testament? The Radical tradition tends to undervalue the Old Testament and/or to regard it as superseded by the New. Anabaptists are hardly alone in this failing—if anything, the Lutheran tradition's hermeneutical elevation of the law-gospel dialectic is even worse—but the matter must be reconsidered in our time. Jesus' teaching and action can be understood rightly only when he is placed firmly in the context of the Judaism of his time and of the longer story of God's dealings with Israel.

Second, I see an unresolved tension in the Anabaptist tradition between authority and freedom. This tension manifests itself in practices of biblical interpretation and in the mechanisms of decision-making in the community's life. In Metanoia Fellowship, for instance, we faced constant struggles about such issues as we tried to pursue decision-making by community consensus under the guidance of the Holy Spirit. The Radical Reformers insisted that they were recalling the faithful to live strictly by what the Bible said, rather than by the body of tradition developed in the church over many centuries. But who is to decide how the Bible is to be interpreted, particularly on contested issues (such as current debates about sexuality)? Is each individual free to decide? How then can there be coherence in the community's life, and how can there be any meaningful practice of church discipline? On the other hand, if the community's leaders guide the church in the process of interpretation, then do the community's decisions take on the status of authoritative traditions that shape the subsequent reading of Scripture? If so, how is this different in principle from what catholic Christianity has always claimed about the authoritative role of tradition? I face this conundrum constantly in my own work as a theologian committed to the authority of Scripture in the church, and the Radical Reformation traditions have not, on the whole, offered any clear resolution of the problem.

These questions and criticisms should be understood as coming from a grateful friend of Radical Reformation theology. I have learned far more from the tradition than I could ever presume to teach it. I continue to find the witness of the Radical Reformation churches inspiring and challenging, and I expect that the power of their testimony will increase in the coming century, as the church in the West comes to grips with its new situation as a disenfranchised minority in a post-Constantinian world.

CHAPTER TWELVE

Anabaptism and the Obstacles That Make for Vocation

Rodney Clapp

"Always be ready to make your defense to anyone who demands from you an accounting for the hope that is in you . . . ." So the First Letter of Peter (3:15) counsels us, and in response I know that much of the hope that is in me is owed to the Anabaptist tradition.

But I am not very prepared to provide that account, even to the extent of saying how I have been challenged and shaped by Anabaptism. I did not grow up in a Mennonite or Brethren or Quaker church, but rather in United Methodism. And even now, as over the course of most of my adult life, I do not worship as an Anabaptist, but as an Episcopalian— which, at least on the surface, would seem to have taken me even further from the influence of Menno and his successors. Yet my writing and other work are clearly and indelibly marked by Anabaptism. Whence the deep chords of resonance? How to explain the profound influence of Anabaptism on my theology and discipleship?

These questions inescapably drive back to vocation, to how God calls a person into and defines a particular life's work. We often, and rightly, think of vocation in terms of gifts and talents, but I am convinced that who we are and what we become are not just a matter of the gifts God gives us but also of the limitations and even inadequacies God refuses to air-lift us out of or away from. Sometimes we find our vocations not so much by following our bliss as by facing obstacles. Hence the fact that I am today a writer and publisher has much to do with the ignominious reality that I almost flunked first grade. I had trouble learning how to read; my mother secured my passage to second grade only by promising the first-grade teacher that she would work with me all summer on my grammar and vocabulary. And so for a few hours every day we worked our way together through countless storybooks. By the beginning of the next school year I had not only learned how to read but had fallen in love with stories and with books. That love of story—and not my brush with illiteracy!—is one aspect of formation that later predisposed me to an appreciation of Anabaptism. Hence, although I would later study philosophy and certainly respectfully use it in my own theological work, I have always found its abstractness and formality something less than adrenaline-producing. The messy and colorful details, the unpredictability and stubborn particularities of narrative, have seemed to me more useful and exciting in making sense out of faith and life. In Anabaptism I have found a Christian tradition resolutely focused on the story of Israel and Jesus Christ and more prone to dig into the gritty soil of history than to take flight on the wings of philosophical speculation.

In retrospect, I think at least one more aspect of situational vocation predisposed me to pay attention to Anabaptism. I grew up in Forgan, Oklahoma, a small agricultural and petroleum-producing town of 400 people, which fostered in me a certain outsider identity in a couple of ways. Being bookish, daydreamy, and unmechanical, I simply did not fit the norm of the practical, common-sensical, born handyman sons of farmers and gas plant mechanics. Not that my childhood was tormented—far from it—but from earliest recollections I never felt like I fully and naturally belonged. I always related to the outsider. The second factor, however, has to do with the fact that I identified with my small-town origins so much that I could not identify with much of the rest of the world. By my early college years I was impressed that, whether or not my townspeople wanted to admit it, rural America was far from the national norm, and even more removed from the centers of real power in U.S. society. I was too young to be threatened by the draft for the Vietnam War, but several town kids only a few years older than I went off to that war. Out of that tiny town, probably a dozen young citizens fought in East Asia, and close to a half dozen never returned or—as in the case of two—returned shellshocked and haunted, and committed suicide in their twenties. Such disproportionalities, and the political impotency to do anything about them, along with the inclination never to disclaim my origins, reinforced in me a tendency to identify with the outsider.

For a variety of reasons—not the least its faithfulness to a Lord who had no place to lay his head and died an outcast's death beyond the city walls—the Anabaptist tradition understands the outsider status. It has only lately—and, thank God, not uniformly—been tempted to think that the church should identify with empire. And it has cultivated the creativity and graceful, nonviolent forms of power that only those not grasping at the reins of conventional, worldly power can desire or be possessed by.

Story and outsiderdom, then, hint at vocational dispositions that both informed my own appropriation of Christian faith and laid tracks on which Anabaptist trains of thought could later run. My first real encounter with that thought occurred early in college, through the reading of *Sojourners* magazine. Surely due in part to its own influence by Anabaptists, the magazine was clearly not fully at home with or "inside" the American dream. And it stubbornly returned to the story of the gospel (as well as other parts of the Bible) to read and interpret the world in which it dwelled. One writer who frequently graced the magazine's pages especially captivated me with his ability to see to the heart of things through biblical lenses. That was John Howard Yoder. I soon learned of a book he had written a few years before, *The Politics of Jesus*, which I promptly read. I recall being impressed by the profound biblical provenance of the book and by the force of its clean, bracing argumentation. But the truth is that I could not then imagine embracing a Christianity that was so radically and confidently itself that it would subordinate the politics of the nation-state to the politics of the church. In other words, I clearly was not so much of an outsider as the brief autobiographical musings above might suggest! I also failed to take to heart Yoder's own insistence that he was writing not just out of and for a single denomination, but for the ecumenical church. It seemed to me that I would have to join a Mennonite church in order really and fairly to take Yoder seriously, and I was not prepared to make such a step—since, rightly or wrongly, and probably some degrees of both, I saw the Mennonite church as an ethnic church.

Fewer than 10 years later, however, in 1985, a second book recast my reading of Yoder and so opened doors on the Anabaptist tradition I formerly thought closed to me. Working as an editor at *Christianity Today*, I noticed a book called *The Peaceable Kingdom* on the review desk. Since I had heard of Stanley Hauerwas, I took the book home to read. *The Peaceable Kingdom* coalesced and catalyzed a number of factors that had become crucial in my life of faith but whose coherence on an intellectual level remained murky to me. One such factor was Hauerwas' emphasis on narrative, which not only fit with my temperamental predilection but took seriously the story-shaped faith of the church and its Bible and showed why, on theo-philosophical grounds, that particularistic narrative should not be abandoned. I had already been assured of this via Barth, but Hauerwas helped me more clearly understand Barth's motivating concerns for the irreplaceable priority of the Word, and he stated the case for biblical narrative more explicitly, in terms more readily related to emerging postmodern epistemological debates. The second coalescing and catalyzing factor was Hauerwas' close attention to and appreciation of the worship life of the church. In the previous few years he had lived among the Catholics at Notre Dame, and taken to heart the power of sacramental liturgy. Just four or five years previously I had been confirmed into the Episcopal Church, out of my own appreciation for eucharistically-centered spirituality. I had known great nourishing and formational richness in the liturgy and sacraments, and in *The Peaceable Kingdom* met exciting theological rationale for such experience. But the third factor that made the book important to me had to do with what I have here referred to as outsider status. Hauerwas called the church not to endorse and anoint the status quo with holy oil, but to claim its unique mission and contradict the world for the world's sake.

This third factor pushed me to reconsider Yoder. Hauerwas was (and is) United Methodist. Perhaps, then, I did not have to join a Mennonite Church in order to learn in good faith from Yoder. I not only reread *The Politics of Jesus,* but also read Yoder's later book *The Priestly Kingdom.* And this time I paid attention to his insistence that he wrote ecumenically, for the church catholic and evangelical. Readings of Yoder's corpus led to literary encounters—and in some especially happy cases, eventual friendship—with other Anabaptist thinkers, including James McClendon, Norman Kraus, Nancey Murphy, Tom Finger, and John Driver. This influence was central in my decision to pursue further theological education at Bethany Seminary, where Dale Brown robustly presented the Anabaptist tradition in all its variegated history and Lauree Hersch Meyer showed how a committed pacifist could love and learn from Augustine.

Anabaptist thought and witness, then, has been at the marrow of my more developed—or at least more explicitly understood—vocation. I am called as a writer and editor to help the church more faithfully understand its distinctive mission, as a community uniquely based on the revelation of God in Israel and Jesus Christ, and consequently in cruciformed service to the world with which God seeks to be reconciled. The Anabaptist tradition is one Christian tradition that has typically understood the church and its mission in just this manner, true to the biblical story and God's own outsiderly empathy for the stranger, the outcast and the forgotten. Consequently, the Anabaptist tradition has worshiped and missionized nonviolently. Thus it has extraordinary accumulated wisdom to share with much of the rest of the western church, which now must through force of circumstances (God's fresh unveiling of Christian vocation?) learn how to be church without assuming that surrounding cultures are already at least latently Christian or can, with the empire's help, be coercively "evangelized."

However indebted as I am to the Anabaptist tradition, and as much as I think the whole church catholic and evangelical has to learn from it, I remain an Episcopalian. At bottom, this has to do with the sacraments and sacramental theology. I fear that Zwinglian memorialistic understandings of baptism and the Lord's Supper all too readily play into individualistic, subjectivistic spiritualities. If these practices are merely occasions for our own mental recollection of Jesus and his sacrificial life and death, then faith (at least here) is a matter of human initiative. Theologically, memorialistic observances run against the grain of prevenient grace—that God, while we were yet lost, first reached out to humanity through and in Israel and Jesus Christ. To the extent that current Anabaptists are Zwinglian, I suspect that their successes in being gracefully gathered and empowered communities occurs in spite of their theology and practice of baptism and eucharist.

Correlatively, I think that Anabaptist missional strategy may on this point have some things to learn from Roman Catholic, Anglican, Lutheran, and other more determinedly sacramental traditions. I mention only one, signal instance: For good and for ill, the world we inhabit is moving out of the age of the word and into the age of the image. For a variety of reasons (and not least as a bookmaker!) I hope the church will not give up on the printed word. But I have no doubt that visual images will assume increased importance in the communication and conduct of Christian life. In corporate worship, for instance, those traditions that emphasize the sacramental (or imaged) Word as well as the proclaimed (spoken or written) Word will more readily appeal to and communicate with people whose existence is suffused with mediated imagery.

In short, the recent hope expressed by ethicist Gerald Schlabach that Catholics be more Anabaptist, Anabaptists more Catholic, and mainline Protestants more of both gets it just about right.[1] That may aptly summarize the vocation of the western church in the twenty-first century.

CHAPTER THIRTEEN

Sharing the House of God: Learning to Read Scripture with Anabaptists

Michael G. Cartwright

A s any long-time participant in ecumenical engagements between diverse Christian traditions knows, it is one thing to locate one's disagreements with another Christian tradition in the context of theological argumentation, and it is quite another thing to locate oneself in relation to flesh-and-blood embodiments of another tradition. Once one discerns the presence of the transformative power of God in other Christian traditions, then one is forced to realign one's conceptual map in humble recognition that one has not yet discerned the "fullness of Christ" (Eph. 4:13 KJV) much less accepted all that could be shared if one were fully open to the Spirit's direction. My intermittent encounters as a child and adult with proponents and practitioners of Anabaptist theology and ethics over the past thirty-five years have repeatedly caused me to re-draw my conceptual map of the *oikon tou theou* ("house of God") as I have come to know a diverse company of Christians from Radical Reformation traditions through common worship, study, argument, and friendship.

As a theological ethicist in the United Methodist tradition, I like to tease my Mennonite friends about the risk they run in "consorting with people who war," as some eighteenth-century Mennonites in Eastern Pennsylvania referred to "the people called Methodist." I am no good judge of whether my engagements with the heirs of Menno Simons, Michael Sattler, and Pilgram Marpeck have thus far done more harm than good. I am quite sure, however, many Mennonites have been—and continue to be—a "means of grace" for me even in the midst of what I take to be some rather significant disagreements about whether it is even necessary to talk about "means of grace" for the formation of Christian disciples. In fact, I not only literally learned to read with Mennonite children, but I have had the opportunity to share "the house" of the church with a variety of Anabaptist friends. Through our association I hope I have learned to be a better reader of scripture, although I cannot make that judgment apart from assessing my ongoing commitment to, and struggles with, the "people called Methodist."

Much of what I have learned in this regard can be located in relation to my interest in John Howard Yoder's theological contributions. When I collected and edited Yoder's *The Royal Priesthood: Essays Ecclesiological and Ecumenical* (1994), I consciously tried to represent Yoder's work to mainline Protestant and Catholic readers. Several years ago, my friend Gerald Schlabach astutely observed that, as a theologian working out of a mainline Protestant tradition, I probably had to put this book together to begin locating my own differences with Yoder in these matters. He was right. I was unable to begin to identify the significance of my differences with Yoder until I worked on that project.

I knew that Yoder and I had strong differences in our understanding of the sacraments. I am much more at home with a theology of "the real presence" of Christ in the eucharist. I also think of baptism as first and foremost God's act in the church, a profound gift of grace to those who are baptized. I am fully aware that this view places me in striking disagreement with many Mennonites, as well as most Christians in Radical Reformation traditions. Mennonites have often expressed surprise that I could be so committed to the recovery of "giving and receiving counsel" and so unrepentant about infant baptism.[1] I understand their incredulity, since Methodists in American culture have been known more for our laxity than for our discipline in such matters. But I argue that baptism makes sense within the context of a "lifelong catechumenate" for all Christians. We grow into our baptism in much the same way that a novice grows into the monk's cowl that he receives upon entering a monastic order.[2] I believe—as Yoder did not believe—that as children of God we are formed for a life of faith through means of grace such as baptism and eucharist.

Discovering the Anabaptist Witness While Learning to Read with Miriam and John

What is this place where we are meeting?
Only a house, the earth its floor.
Walls and a roof sheltering people,
windows for light, an open door.
Yet, it becomes a body that lives
when we are gathered here,
and know our God is near.[3]

Oddly enough, my earliest encounters with Anabaptists occurred thirty-five years ago on Sunday afternoons at the West Richwoods Community Building on Highway 9 in Stone County, Arkansas. My father was pastor of First Baptist Church in the county seat town of Mountain View. Twice a week he preached for the Baptist congregation that met in the Richwoods Community Building, and I sometimes tagged along when he preached for this smaller congregation. Coincidentally, the local (Conservative) Mennonite congregation also worshiped in that same building on Sunday afternoons. The Mennonites left the building shortly before 2 p.m., at which time the Baptists took possession of the building for a hour or so of fiery preaching in quest of intense spiritual awakening.

Not grasping the shared use of the community building, at that time I assumed that the Mennonites were renting space from the Baptist congregation. I can remember wondering: How can you have a church without a building? Even though I had already learned to sing the little children's ditty (with hand motions)—"Here's the church, Here's the steeple, Open the doors, Where's the people?"—the effect of which was to remind children that "church" does not refer primarily to the building. I also knew that buildings could be and often were the subject of controversy in the world of Southern Baptists. By the time I was eight years old in 1965, I already knew of several nearby congregations that had split over questions of building and expansion.

I don't recall ever being in the Richwoods Community Building when the Mennonite congregation was actually using it, and I doubt that I was even curious about their worship services at the time. I do not recall the building looking much different from most other country churches of Arkansas at which my father occasionally preached—a plain wooden structure with plank pews and a clock on the wall to remind the preacher when it was time to go home. What I do recall, however, is that I was amazed that this congregation had so few automobiles. Although I am sure that there were several cars, at the time it seemed to me that there was only one car for the whole church.

The father of John Mast, my elementary school playmate, was the pastor of the Mennonite congregation. John and I would greet each other as his congregation was leaving and the Baptist congregation was arriving. John's father would load seven or eight people in his old gray International Harvester station wagon to carry them home after church. Sometimes people had to wait until he could take the first load home and come back and get others. I can remember being puzzled by this. "Don't all Americans own cars?" I wondered. Mennonites seemed foreign to me because of this.

A town known more for the diversity of views about the consumption of alcohol[4] than for the diversity of its religious communities of faith, Mountain View was made up mostly of Baptists and Methodists, with some Pentecostal churches beginning to make their presence known. Had there been a Catholic church in Mountain View, it would probably have been known for the "wet" views of its parishioners rather than for anything having to do with its sacramental theology. At that time the world seemed to be composed of Baptists and "the others."

Methodists seemed to be the chief rivals to Baptist dominance, and I was raised to believe that everyone knew that they drank alcohol as much as Catholics did, although I had also heard that some of those Methodists had "gone holiness" and were tee-totallers. I couldn't make much sense of Methodists, but Mennonites were even more difficult to locate in relation to my experience, especially since they too practiced a kind of "believer's baptism" but, for reasons that I did not know or understand, Baptists did not "fellowship" with these Christians, nor they with us.

I did know that Southern Baptists emphasized the importance of transformed lives in accordance with Romans 12:1-2 as a way of reinforcing the ethics of personal purity that we were taught—"Don't drink, don't chew, don't go to movies, don't dance, don't fornicate, and don't go with girls that do"—but Southern Baptists in the hills of Arkansas definitely drew the line at counter-cultural practices like simple living, mutual aid, and pacifism. There were *limits* to Christian non-conformity, it seemed. In a county that reputedly had only two African-American citizens, racial integration was virtually a non-issue for people in Mountain View and surrounding communities.

During the week, I went to school with two (Conservative) Mennonite children at Mountain View Elementary School. Miriam Miller, John Mast and I were learning to read books together in Mrs. Morrison's class. Other students in the class regarded John and Miriam as "different." They stood out from the rest of the kids, not so much because of the clothes that they wore—Miriam's dresses were longer than those of the other girls in our class; John's shirts were a bit more somber in color than those that other boys wore—but because of the way they acted during recess. Although not yet baptized members of their respective Mennonite churches, Miriam and John already displayed the practices of peaceableness and humility.

The three of us clearly had some things in common. Miriam and I both loved to read books, although we had different interests. Also, I must have felt some affinity for John since we both were "preachers' kids." I do not remember ever talking with John and Miriam about the Bible as such, although I do remember conversations with Miriam about how many verses of the Bible we each had committed to memory in the past year. We were both proud that we were beginning to read the Bible by ourselves, although we both stumbled over a lot of words, especially in the Old Testament.

Although I am not unaware of the dangers of nostalgia in remembrance of things past,[5] I am reasonably sure that my encounters with Miriam and John were not only my first encounters with Mennonites, but also my first encounter with a discernibly different way of being Christian, and one that posed a positive challenge to my own emerging conception of discipleship. On the playground, as Miriam and John and I played games with the rest of the children, we sometimes fell into conversations that were unlike my conversations with other children.

Long before I ever read John Yoder's classic essay "What Would You Do If?" I recall Miriam asking me questions that gently but firmly suggested that perhaps getting into a fight with the other third-grade boys was not the only option open to me. Probably neither Miriam nor I would have thought of this as "fraternal admonition," but I did have some sense that Miriam was urging me to live by the apostolic mandates to "be ye kind one to another, tenderhearted, forgiving one another, even as God for Christ's sake hath forgiven you" (Eph. 4:32 KJV))—one of the first Bible verses that I memorized. I also recall wondering about why at recess John managed to avoid getting into fights that I seemed to invite. John seemed to act like a "preacher's boy" should behave, whereas I could never quite live up to the idealized image of the pastor's son that was then taking shape in my psyche.

Actually, my most vivid memories of that period are not of children on the playground or teachers in the classroom but rather the books that I was reading at the time. Shortly before my family moved to Mountain View, I had proudly completed reading *John F. Kennedy and the PT-109*—the first book that I picked out by myself to read from the limited stock in the bookmobile that visited the rural hamlet where we lived in the summer of 1965. When we moved to Mountain View in September of that year, I quickly began making my way to the Stone County Library on the second floor of the courthouse on the town square. I still remember the wonder of having access to so many books. In one corner of the library, three shelves held a set of children's biographies. That year, I must have read every volume in the *Famous Americans* series of biographies. Only much later would I realize how strongly these formulaic "storyographies" (192 pages, each with patriotic themes) contributed to my formation as an American citizen and my deformation as a would-be disciple of Christ.

The two years that our family lived in Mountain View, Arkansas, were marked by many events that in retrospect appear to me more significant than I would have realized at the time. During this period my life-long habit of omnivorous reading began, a practice that to this day still shapes my pursuit of those twin passions: "the love of learning and the desire for God." I received my own Bible as a Christmas gift from my parents'—black leather binding with the words of Jesus in red-ink—and began to use the Bible on Sunday nights in Baptist Training Union activities such as the "Bible Sword Drill" competitions. Before I ever learned how to use the Bible for peaceable ends, I was taught that the Bible was a weapon to be used in spiritual warfare with the world.

Shortly before, I had joined the RAs ("Royal Ambassadors for Christ") and began to climb "the mountain" of Christian discipleship as a "squire" seeking to become a "knight" of faith en route to conquest, all of which turned out to coincide with practices of good citizenship. Long before I ever learned about the Protestant and Catholic legacies of Constantinianism, I was living in a world in which Christian discipleship and American citizenship fit hand-in-glove. At the same time, I was given a rich image of Christian discipleship in the metaphor of "royal ambassador" for Christ (2 Cor. 5:17-20), which even today informs my sense of being a scholar-priest who tries to cross borders (and disciplines) within both church and academy in the attempt to bring about change, renewal, and greater understanding in both spheres.

In 1967 I finally "got saved"—after living "under conviction" for five or six months. In fact, I was the last boy in the third grade Sunday school class to profess faith in Christ, a source, as I recall, of some embarrassment, given that I was the preacher's son! On April 23, 1967, I was baptized by my father at First Baptist Church in Mountain View. Later that spring, for the first time, I participated in the Lord's Supper—in the form of a broken saltine cracker and a little shot glass of Welch's grape juice passed to me on an aluminum tray for the first time. At the time, I could not have had any idea that the eucharist would become very important to my understanding of myself as an ordained minister, as well as for my understanding of what the church can and must be in order to fulfill its mission to the world.

I would like to think that this was also the time in my life when I first began to wrestle with what it meant to be a disciple of Jesus Christ in the midst of a host of social tensions that surround us in American culture. But I do not think I really began to question my heritage in any significant way until a year or so later when another series of events unfolded. In the context of turmoil in both my family and the nation, I began to awaken to the deeper effects of hypocrisy in American Christianity—especially with respect to racism.

But in the mid-1960s I was only beginning to recognize the potential questions that I would later have to confront in order to be faithful to the Gospel of Jesus Christ.

In ways that I could never begin to articulate then or now, I was uncomfortably aware that on some levels the Christian witness of these strange Mennonites was more consistently faithful than my own fledgling witness for Christ. I knew that Methodists and Baptists were divided along the lines of infant baptism versus believer's baptism, but I was a bit puzzled about why Mennonites and Baptists regarded one another with unease, even though they did not seem to disagree about baptism. To my eight-year-old mind, Mennonites seemed to be this "third thing" that somehow was neither Protestant (as I experienced it) or Catholic (about which I was fairly ignorant at that time although my mother's family was Catholic).[6]

This circumstance was made all the more awkward by my discovery years later that part of the reason my family had moved to the community of Mountain View was so that I would not have to participate in the integration of public schools in the small community where we had been living in Southern Arkansas. In both subtle and blatant ways, the Southern Baptist congregations of my childhood conveyed to me that I was to be a "royal ambassador" for Jesus Christ *to white people.* At the same time, my encounters with John and Miriam led me to wonder about such lines being drawn in the communities in which my family lived.

The Mennonite congregation that I observed coming and going to church had consistent integrity. To be sure, my encounters with Mennonites over the years have taught me that they have their own kinds of bickering, their own patterns of inter-ethnic rivalry and exclusivity, and their own versions of "people who war." I do admire the Anabaptist vision of the church that provides such a radical way of expressing what it means to be "royal ambassadors for Christ"—with or without a building to call their own, and regardless of the modes of transportation available to them.

My teenage years were filled with more turbulence. I spent the summer I turned fifteen helping to build a building for a mission church (that my father had helped to found), only to see the church split over whether to install central heating and air conditioning. My father left the ministry and subsequently our family declared bankruptcy and my parents were divorced. During my junior year in high school we discovered that my father was afflicted with a mental illness that manifested itself in severely dissociative ways. In the midst of the chaos unfolding in our family, I began to engage some of the social issues of the early 1970s in more self-critical ways. I became more aware of racism, and ultimately committed myself to becoming a "royal ambassador for Christ" to all persons—not just to Euro-Americans like myself. After a period of rebellion at the age of eighteen, I recommitted myself to Christ, was re-baptized—thereby in some sense becoming an *Ana*baptist of a certain kind—and re-engaged the journey of Christian discipleship.

Learning to Read the Bible and History with John Howard Yoder

Words from afar, stars that are falling,
sparks that are sown in us like seed.
Names for our God, dreams, signs and wonders
sent from the past are what we need.
We in this place remember and speak
again what we have heard,
God's free redeeming word.[7]

Rediscovering God's Free Redeeming Word

Words both "near and far" have shaped my life for the past thirty-five years. I sometimes tell people that a good description of what I do is that I am a "wordsmith"—I do things with words in the hope of making a difference. My love of words is distinguishable from my practice of reading scripture, but I will never be able to separate the two. I love the poetry of the Psalms, whether chanted by the monks of St. Meinrad's Archabbey, where I often go on silent retreat, or as sung in the context of the Academy for Spiritual Formation, in which it has been my privilege to teach. There is no better way for me to offer myself to God in the morning than to sing the words of Psalm 63, and there is no greater privilege than to be able to serve as celebrant at the Eucharist of the church. I also enjoy standing in the company of the faithful as together we sing hymns of praise in response to the gracious initiatives of the God who redeems.

I also love the poetry and play of words on the printed page. It is probably no accident that calligraphy is my only hobby—other than reading novels. During my college years I found numerous opportunities to indulge my hunger for books, often devouring five or six books a week in addition to my undergraduate studies. I also had a growing conviction that I was being called to serve God as an ordained minister, at the same time that I yearned to study literature, theology, and ethics. My vocational journey was shaped by the struggle to unite "the love of learning and the desire for God" while learning to live in both the church and the academy.

No longer able to live within the confines of the fundamentalist and racist views of the Southern Baptist congregations of my youth, I found my way into the United Methodist Church through the gracious hospitality of several good friends, college chaplains and pastors, and through reading the theological writings of John Wesley. From the beginning I was convinced that Wesley was right in seeking to conjoin the practice of "speaking the truth in love" in disciplined accountability while also advising the people called Methodist to avail themselves of every opportunity to experience the "ordinary" means of grace—particularly the sacrament of the Eucharist—by which God empowers his people for mission. I also began to discover the hymns of Charles Wesley, which were suffused with the language of scripture. The words of one of Wesley's hymns for Pentecost—"unite the pair so long disjoined, knowledge and vital piety"—came to mean a great deal to me in my vocational self-understanding as a scholar-priest. Learning to embody this unity, of course, has been a lifelong struggle, not simply because of the challenges posed in the academy but also because of the pitfalls that one finds in the church itself.

In 1979 I began seminary at Duke Divinity School, where I continued to relish the opportunities for "the love of learning and the desire for God" that a university setting made possible. Shortly before, I read a doctoral dissertation by J. Denny Weaver that explored some of the tangled history of Protestant disputation about the interpretation of the Bible. I immediately recognized that Weaver was mining veins that I knew that I also wanted to explore, even if I found myself asking a different set of questions than this Mennonite theologian was pressing. I felt an intellectual kinship with Weaver, since I wanted to combine the careful historical reconstruction with a constructive theological agenda. At Duke Divinity School I discovered a faculty that provided worthy role models of erudition at the same time that I continued to discern the shape of my calling to combine scholarship with priestly service to the church.

In retrospect, given my conflicted ecclesial background and the ideological struggles that surrounded my formation as a Christian disciple, it is not surprising that I aspired to do graduate study on the "problem" of the use of scripture in Christian ethics. As I have noted on other occasions, the full story of the influence that John H. Yoder's *Politics of Jesus* has had on mainline Protestant theologians is a history yet to be told. When narrated, one of the plot lines will surely be the ways in which this book helped a new generation of theologians recover and reappropriate "God's free redeeming word" in a circumstance in which "mainline" Protestant traditions have been on the verge of collapse, having already used up the evangelical capital that previous generations had mined so fervently in response to God's initiatives.

Learning the "Resourceful Selectivity" of Being a Scribe of the Kingdom

As a seminarian at Duke Divinity School, I discovered Yoder's *The Politics of Jesus* while working in a bookstore in Durham in 1980. I cannot begin to say how strongly this book resonated with me, or the questions that it posed for me as a "scholar-priest" in training. I recall seeking out one of my professors to ask if he knew of any scholars who had addressed Yoder's interpretations of Jesus's life and ministry. Again, I found that I had to go beyond what I had been taught. Yoder helped me to question modernist paradigms of interpretation and, in effect, gave me the first opportunity to exercise "the suspicion of suspicion," to invoke Rowan Williams' marvelous phrase. In *The Politics of Jesus* I discovered the possibility of dealing with Lessing's "broad ugly ditch" of history without retreating into a posture of anti-intellectualist readings of the Bible or succumbing to an arrogant, all-knowing modernism.

Yoder explained the role to be played by "Agents of Memory" as described in Matthew 13:52—"Every scribe who has been trained for the kingdom of heaven is like a master of a household who brings out of his treasure what is new and what is old." In Yoder's understanding of this metaphor, the scribe "does not speak on his own but as the servant of a community and of the communal memory. Whether the "treasures" which he brings to awareness be ancient or recent, they need to be brought out by someone who is acquainted with the storeroom, and who knows what to bring out when."[8] I have often wondered about the understated character of Yoder's description of this role. Yoder says almost nothing about what is involved in becoming "acquainted" with the storeroom. If I read Yoder correctly, knowing what to bring out when is not so much a skill to be developed in the sense of Aristotle's "practical wisdom" as it is God-given wisdom made available to the church at a particular moment in time through the activity of the Holy Spirit. This image of "the householder's gift of resourceful selectivity" also lies at the heart of Yoder's conception of what it means to enact "the hermeneutics of peoplehood."

Learning the "Hermeneutics of Peoplehood"

As a graduate student, the more I read Yoder's work, the more profound my engagement with the Anabaptist tradition became. The day that I read Yoder's essay "A People in the World" in my carrel in the basement of the Divinity School Library at Duke University was the day that I discovered a hermeneutical insight that made it possible for me to launch my own proposals for how Protestants can go about re-engaging Scripture:

> The work of God is the calling of a people. . . . The church then is not simply the bearer of a message of reconciliation, in the way a newspaper or telephone company can bear any message with which it is entrusted. Nor is the church simply the result of a message, as an alumni association is the product of the school or the crowd in the theater is the product of the reputation of the film. That men and women are called together into a new social wholeness is itself the work of God, which gives meaning to history, from which both personal conversion (whereby individuals are called into this meaning) and missionary instrumentalities are derived.[9]

Yoder's argument, which he would always contend was nothing more or less than a careful reading of Ephesians 3:10, made it possible for me to bring into focus some aspects of my own (adopted) Wesleyan heritage that up until then had remained in awkward tension. This passage also prompted further reflection about what it means to form Christians who will embody this "new social wholeness"—a question that Yoder did not address (to my satisfaction) in that essay and that, outside of a few unpublished writings about higher education, I do not think was ever addressed by him in any thorough way.

No doubt the fact that I studied with Stanley Hauerwas at the Graduate School of Duke University (1985-88) provided a kind of "intellectual cover" for my interest in what I came to regard as Yoder's "communal hermeneutic," but I think I would have continued to read Yoder's work anyway. At the time, Yoder's work was one of the few ways that I could find for reconstructing an "ecclesial hermeneutic" for Christian ethics.[10] Assisted by William Klassen's exemplary historical scholarship,[11] I would learn more about the history of "communal hermeneutics" in the Anabaptist tradition, especially as found in the work of Pilgram Marpeck, whose contribution to Anabaptist theology and ethics remains underappreciated in my opinion. Without reading Yoder, I probably would never have read Sattler, Marpeck, Hubmaier, et al., much less discovered how to argue the case I wanted to make for prescriptive uses of scripture in Christian ethics.

Learning to "Loop Back" by Pruning the Vine

From Yoder, I also learned the significance of engaging the Christian tradition by "looping back" while taking seriously the formative dimensions of the Christian tradition:

> Far from being an ongoing growth like a tree (or family tree), the wholesome growth of tradition is like a vine: a story of constant interruption of growth in favor of pruning and a new chance for roots. This renewed appeal to origins is not primitivism, nor an effort to recapture some pristine purity. It is rather a "looping back," a glance over the shoulder to enable a midcourse correction, a rediscovery of something from the past whose pertinence was not seen before, because only a new question or challenge enables us to see it speaking to us. To stay with the vinedresser's image, the effect of pruning is not to harm the vine, but to provoke new growth out of the old wood nearer to the ground, to decrease the loss of food and time along the sap's path from the roots to the fruit, and to make the grapes easier to pick. *Ecclesia reformata semper reformanda* is not really a statement about the earlier tradition's permanent accessibility, as witnessed to and normed by Scripture in its nucleus, but always including more dimensions than the Bible itself contains, functioning as an instance of appeal as we call for renewed faithfulness and denounce renewed apostasy. The

most important operational meaning of the Bible for ethics is not that we do just what it says in some way that we can derive deductively. It is rather that we are able, thanks to the combined gifts of teachers and prophets, to become aware that we do not do what it says, and that the dissonance we thereby create enables our renewal.[12]

For Yoder, then, the "authority" of the tradition exists only insofar as or so long as Christians continue to read scripture in a "never-ending conversation" with the awareness that it is God's free redeeming word that authorizes the conversation.

Although Yoder is more correct than not in this matter, I found him to be somewhat oblivious to the role played by factors other than intellectual argumentation in forming and sustaining those who would participate in such a reading community. In this respect, I have been much more interested than Yoder ever was in exploring the roles played (positively and negatively) by such things as the sacraments as well as the whole realm of what is now called "material culture" in the formation and deformation of Christians—whether at the level of the congregation or in denominational family sagas that link the peoplehood of contemporary Christians with the peoplehood of Israel and the first Christian communities.

Of course, this contention does not mean that Yoder had no interest in re-framing discussions of the sacraments. On the contrary, he made a significant contribution to explaining the social processes that the sacraments, properly understood, can be said to embody. Yet even Yoder's most promising discussions of "sacrament as social process" tended to be a more erudite and elaborate form of Zwinglianism. Yoder's typology of "sacramental realism," as distinguished from the "sacramentalist" and rationalistic Zwinglian types,[13] is a bit misleading insofar as it can be read to suggest that Yoder was not still working out of a kind of Zwinglian sensibility. Yoder's attempt to identify a middle position between the extremes of "rationalistic Zwinglians" and "sacramentalists" is more than a little tendentious and ultimately not convincing.

Knowing the historical background of this distinction does not help me to resolve the matter. In his essay "A People in the World," Yoder discusses what he regarded as "the classical options" in terms of a three-cornered triangle of the theocratic, spiritualist, and believers' church options. At one corner, Yoder locates the believers' church vision of Anabaptism as best exemplified by Michael Sattler and Pilgram Marpeck, both of whom sought "to carry to its logical conclusion the Reformation principle of the restoration of original conclusion Christianity. . . ." Spiritualists like Caspar Schwenckfeld and theocratic humanists such as Huldrich Zwingli occupy the other two corners. As Yoder notes, Zwingli appealed to the text of Matthew 15:13—"Every plant that my heavenly Father has not planted will be uprooted," in his arguments against Johannes Faber. This same text was used by Anabaptists against Zwingli.[14]

Yoder provided an extended discussion of this particular position in a footnote that I find illuminating precisely because it attempted to sort out the senses in which Anabaptist hermeneutics were governed by *sola scriptura*. "Anabaptists coupled the appeal to Scripture with an accent on the 'Inner Word,' analogous to the Quaker concept of 'Christ's coming to teach his people today.' Thus the issue is the authority of Christ versus the authority of humans, not the Christ of Scripture versus the present Christ."[15] I do not know of a place in Yoder's writing where he explicitly renounces this Zwinglian conception of the "Inner Word." Nor do I know of any place where Yoder offered a more nuanced assessment. What Yoder leaves us with, then, is a radically *synchronic* understanding of both the Word of God and the church as a gathered community of faith. In sum, Yoder thought that at any given time in human history, God's Holy Spirit could constitute a community of faith around the Word of God read and proclaimed, but Yoder's conception of tradition simply did not permit diachronic continuity.

While Yoder's essay and subsequent book *Body Politics* both provide a wonderful explication of the social dimension of the gathered community, I find these accounts still captive to a Zwinglian sensibility. Namely, there is no mystery to be discerned in these actions. Yoder simply was not willing (or able) to recognize that God may also work through human mediations that occur in space and time to constitute the church. For Yoder, like Zwingli, "human traditions" are by definition unfaithful traditions, and must be "uprooted." By contrast, Yoder regards "original traditions" to be those that "enshrine the commandments of God" as found in Scripture.[16] One can affirm with Yoder that "real presence" occurs in the Eucharist as well as in feeding the hungry, in baptism as well as in hospitality.[17] At the same time, one need not concede that the church must be formed by particular means of grace, such as the Eucharist, precisely so that Christians can learn to see the "real presence" of Christ in the stranger who is housed as well as to discover the hospitality that makes it possible for us to give ourselves in feeding the hungry.

Yoder's notion of "sacrament as social process" has marked the way that I do theological ethics in profound ways. For example, I have advocated the restoration of practices such as "foot washing" among mainline Protestant communities of faith, thanks to what I learned from Yoder's work. In accounting for the importance of this practice, however, I would be much more inclined to agree with St. Bernard of Clairvaux that it is a profound "sacrament" for the church,[18] whereas Yoder sees its significance as the enactment of service, the underlying anthropology of which is to "subject my freedom for the need of my brother or sister."[19] Like St. Bernard of Clairvaux, I believe that the washing of feet *signifies* things—in time and space—that make it possible for us to experience forgiveness while also being empowered for service. It is both unnecessary and unhelpful to regard such complexes of meaning as merely "human traditions," since such practices constitute amazing opportunities for transformation in the midst of our own woundedness with respect to our capacity for relationship and love.[20]

Rethinking the Role of Worship in Yoder's Ecclesiology

This set of issues leads to the question of how Yoder understood the role of worship. An instrumentalist account of worship in Christian formation floats through Yoder's corpus of writing alongside other discussions of the "doxological community" that I find much more suggestive. Yoder's synchronic analysis of the church leads him to offer the kind of "schematic summary of the marks of the church" that focuses on eight specific functions or "notae," with a view toward unfolding the social processes of these "sacramental forms."[21] For example, in the "Hermeneutics of Peoplehood" essay cited above, Yoder provides an account of the relationship between liturgy and ethics that is as fascinating for what it excludes as well as for what it asserts:

> Neither in the New Testament documents nor in radical Protestantism is there a discretely identifiable function called "priesthood" or a specific activity called "worship." The function which created the synagogue in central diaspora Judaism was the scribal one of reading the holy writings. What we call "worship" is hard to locate as the task of one officer. Breaking bread in the solemn memory of the Lord's suffering and the joyous acclamation of his presence and promised return was one of the things both the early Christians and the radical Protestants did regularly, but they needed no special officers for that. It was more such action that constituted them as "church" than were the sending out of missionaries, the collection of famine relief moneys or practical moral reasoning.[22]

Setting aside the issue of whether Yoder's assessment of the New Testament writings is correct, I question Yoder's claim that worship is *not* constitutive for Christian identity and community. But before I proceed in that direction, I must also call attention to other places where Yoder discussed worship in ways that point in different directions.

For example, much of Yoder's work resulted from assignments and invitations to address issues of moral and theological import. Rarely was Yoder called upon to address questions of Christian spiritual formation, and he did so only in the context of conference addresses for church-related higher education. If any of these were published, they were not published separately but as part of a larger effort in which his own words mingled with the contributions of others.

One rather enigmatic exception is the concluding paragraph of "Back to True North" in which Yoder briefly identifies what "an authentic portrayal" of the peace church vision would have focused on if the topic had been addressed in terms that did not skew the description as a result of engaging the issues posed by "dialogue with majority mentalities." Yoder observes that such an account "from the inside would have spoken more of worship and servanthood, reconciliation and creativity, *Gelassenheit* and the Power of the Light, 'heartfelt religion' and transforming hope, and the person of Jesus Christ."[23]

This passage from *The Priestly Kingdom* is tantalizing yet ultimately elusive given that Yoder never actually offers such an account in any of his published or unpublished writings. In fact, Yoder himself studiously avoided using language about the constitutive significance of worship and the sacraments as "means of grace."[24] Yoder always stressed the *political* significance of worship. On one occasion he pointedly stated, "Worship is the communal cultivation of an alternative structure of society and of history."[25] Although I want to agree with Yoder's statement, I believe that the means to the political end he describes lies in the constitutive role played by the sacraments and other ordinary means of grace that God provides to gather the community. Yoder was always mistrustful of such conceptual moves precisely because he thought they end up serving to justify Constantinian accommodations of the church, and too often they formed the framework of questions that have been used by Protestant and Catholic scholastics as weapons to subjugate or delegitimize Anabaptists past and present.

Even after seeing Yoder's conception of sacrament as social process in context, I confess that Yoder's account of sacramentality strikes me as oddly one-dimensional,[26] as if the only human faculty shaped by God's grace is the intellect and the only way we are present to and with one another is through the use of words. Surely this is not the case. But that is the outcome of Yoder's overtly *kerygmatic* focus in his various reflections on sacrament as social process. I argue, by contrast, that the formation, deformation and reformation of the church always take place in the context of practices that involve the full range of human senses and capacities for participation. In this respect, sometimes I have wondered if Yoder forgot that reading is itself a social practice into which people are initiated, and that it is formed through the senses not only in the house of God but also in the schoolhouse and the library, spaces for which Yoder and I both shared a great love and appreciation.

After all my years of study and teaching, I still marvel at the capacity of words to transform the lives of students in those rare moments when education actually happens. I continue to stand amazed on those occasions when the Word of God is read and proclaimed in the context of the community of faith. Indeed, at a time when the Word of the Lord once again seems rare, I give thanks for the story of Samuel, to whom God promised that the Word of the Lord would be enacted in such a powerful way that it would "make both ears of anyone who hears of it tingle" (1 Sam. 3:11). What a wonderful metaphor for the sensory delight that "God's free redeeming word" makes possible for the people of God within the constraints of human history. The Word of God that comes to us does not require that we divorce ourselves from our other senses and rely on intellect alone.

Herein lies a critical difference between Yoder's neo-Anabaptist conception of "sacrament as social process" and those of us who stand within sacramental traditions. For Yoder, regardless of the practices that are embodied before the eyes of the watching world, the Word of God can only be experienced as an "Inner Word" to which the gathered community of faith testifies, whereas for Protestants like John Wesley and John Calvin as well as for those who stand within the Roman Catholic tradition, the Word of God is believed to come to us in audible forms such as preaching and is made visible in sacraments like the Eucharist.

The Vocation of the Theological Ethicist Living in the Midst of Unstable Syntheses

And we accept bread at his table,
broken and shared, a living sign.
Here in this world, dying and living
We are each other's bread and wine.

This is the place where we can receive
what we need to increase.
God's justice and God's peace. [27]

One of the strange features of contemporary Christianity is that one often finds oneself in ecclesial contexts where there is a "disconnect" between what one might expect to be the case, based on denominational history and geographical location, and what actually transpires in a given gathering of would-be Christians. These disjunctions between theory and practice place theological ethicists in an interesting circumstance, not only because we may find ourselves in situations where our discriminating use of words to describe the moral life may fail to do justice to the richness of what is transpiring in a given Christian community, but also because the words we use, "whatever their intention or precision," may have effects that we cannot predict. This is one reason why I regard both contemporary Anabaptist and contemporary Methodist theologies as constituting an unstable syntheses.

Rediscovering Methodism Through the "Believers" Church

Although Donald Durnbaugh and Franklin Littell addressed this topic more directly, Yoder's work has enabled me to understand better the senses in which Methodism as a movement may or may not be regarded as part of the believers' church tradition.[28] As I have written elsewhere, American Methodist ecclesiology, like the vision of the church held by its "founder," John Wesley, is an "unstable blend of Anabaptist and Anglican ecclesiologies."[29] At least part of that instability can be described as a "daring" attempt to synthesize a robust practice of church discipline with a vital sacramental theology. At our best, Methodists have exercised our "ecumenical vocation" to be an "evangelical order within . . . the church catholic" whose charism is holiness.[30] At our worst, Methodists have displayed some of the worst errors of Constantinian triumphalism, as well as a studied disregard for using theological and moral language in undisciplined ways. Methodists have preferred to exercise the arts of equivocation and accommodation rather than the plain and simple practices of "Christian conference" in seeking to fulfill the apostolic mandate to "spread scriptural holiness across the land. . . ."

Yoder' work has helped me understand the significance of Wesley's "unstable synthesis," but my understanding of the importance of the sacraments as a means of grace has helped me to see how the Mennonite-Anabaptist tradition could also be regarded as an unstable synthesis. Whatever the merits of Yoder's ecumenical Neo-Anabaptist theology of the sacraments as "social process," it does not account for all that goes on in the typical Mennonite or Methodist congregation when they are most faithfully carrying out their mission to embody the gospel as social ethics. Yoder's emphasis on the gathered community does provide for the formation of disciples or the formation of community as such. Yoder can explain what church looks like, when it happens, but he does not bother to describe how it comes into being over time. Hence the instability of his synthesis with respect to the question of how to cultivate communal discipline and how to form faithful disciples.

I am intrigued by Yoder's retrospective descriptions of the ferment within the Mennonite Church as a denomination in the 1960s. Yoder apparently perceived the internal debate within the denomination at that time as being "about whether to be the 'established' religious expression of a small culture, a mini-christendom, or whether to be a church only of adult believers."[31] Yoder could not imagine the possibility of a non-established church sustained by the discipline of a lifelong catechumenate enabled by disciplined use of the means of grace. This is a United Methodist perspective on the "third way" excluded by Yoder. Apparently he did not think it possible to have a disciplined company of believers grounded in the sacraments of baptism, the Eucharist, and other practices. And that in turn shaped what Yoder thought was the proper task of theological ethics as practiced in the church and academy.

The Vocation of the Theological Ethicist

As a graduate student at Duke University in the mid-1980s, I participated in a "pro-seminar" discussing "The Vocation of the Theologian." Graduate students made presentations on the work of various theologians, some of whom saw a very tight bond between the work of the theologian and the work of the church, and others of whom did not find this to be a particularly helpful connection for their theological endeavors. Although I do not recall that we read Yoder's work in that seminar, I do know that Yoder, perhaps more than any other theologian, has pushed me to think about my own vocation as a theological ethicist.

Yoder articulated his conception of the vocation of the theological ethicist at various times during the last decade of his life. One of the most fully articulated statements is found in his Presidential address to the Society of Christian Ethics in 1988 at Duke University, "To Serve Our God and Rule the

World," which engages a discussion of "Liturgy and Ethics" that had emerged within that scholarly guild in the 1970s.[32] The lecture begins with the hymn of the four animals in Rev. 5:7-10 and concludes with the hymn of all creation in Rev. 5:13-14. Yoder explains the sixfold sense in which Christians or Christian ethicists should "see history doxologically." Space does not permit me to summarize the elaborate and carefully nuanced way that Yoder describes "the doxological community" as it exists against the eschatological backdrop of human history, but I do want to explain the complex metaphor Yoder uses to describe the role of "the agent of moral discernment in the context of the doxological community."

Yoder pointedly reminded his colleagues in the Society of Christian Ethics:

> The agent of moral discernment is not a theologian, a bishop, or a pollster, but the Holy Spirit, discerned as the unity of the entire body.
>
> The lifeblood of that body is language. When the ability of human blood to carry its freight is threatened by an antigen, the type B lymphocytes produce antibodies to fit that specific invader. The lymphocytes' function has no indepen-dent merit. While the body is healthy they are not needed. There is no use for the antibodies before the antigen invades, although their traces stay in the system after the disease is over. Our guild's vocation is vigilance against the abuse of words or of the logic of the discerning community. We are neither the umpires nor the examiners, the bishops nor the catechists, the evangelists nor the moderators. We are the immune system of the language flow that keeps the body going.[33]

Immediately following this metaphor of the vocation of the theological ethicist as "immune system of the body" Yoder invokes two additional images, two more ways of saying the same thing. The first image is that of scribes of the kingdom or "agents of community memory, selecting from a too-full treasury what just happens to fit the next question."[34]

In line with the immune system image, the exercise of "resourceful selectivity" is not to be regarded as in any sense an act of innovation or virtuosity, but rather as redirection or correction in the interest of remaining faithful to the gospel. The second is that of heralds or "ecumenical runners, carrying from one world to another the word of what has been suffered, learned, celebrated, confessed elsewhere."[35] This apparently is the role of "royal ambassadors for Christ" who understand that the message they bring to the cultures to which they are sent ultimately cannot be separated from the work of reconciliation that must be embodied in the gathered community of faith.

While I resonate with Yoder's imagery as well as his description of the vocation of the theologian, I worry a bit about the degree to which Yoder's imagery does not appear to provide for the formation of the theologian, particularly given the strong sense in which academic culture shapes theological ethicists. At least some Anabaptists, some of the time, must have had profoundly sacramental sensibilities in the sense that they lived daily life in the awareness of the Holy Spirit pervading all things, ranging from daily tasks of work to the humble service expressed in the plain and simple act of washing one another's feet. And I am not unaware of the rich ways in which *Gelassenheit* (yieldedness) is embodied by Christians in various Anabaptist traditions.[36]

I question, however, whether Yoder's attempt to provide an updated and somewhat more cosmopolitan account of Anabaptist sacramental understanding can ultimately be sustained by contemporary Mennonite congregations without a stronger conception of the role played by the means of grace. If in their "dying and living" the gathered community is to "be each other's bread and wine," then they will need to be able to interpret these "living signs." I find it very curious that the hymn "What Is This Place" uses the metaphors of the sacraments to describe the community, even though Anabaptists do not have the kind of sacramental theology that supports such a conception of real presence. It is precisely at this point that I—as a theological ethicist in the United Methodist tradition—find myself arguing that surely it is possible to have a "both/and" and not an "either/or" in this matter.

As much as I concur with Yoder's view of the ongoing necessity of pruning, I also believe in the necessity of spiritual formation. It takes time and is perpetually vulnerable to all kinds of abuses and the possibilities of syncretistic influences. But as Stephen Fowl has convincingly argued, "Christians' prospects for avoiding failure in regard to material practices are related to their refusal to allow these practices to become simply matters of individual concern and private choice. This can only happen as they form, nurture, and maintain the sort of common life that allows these material concerns to become issues for the community as a whole."[37] According to Fowl, participation in Christian practices such as the Eucharist, foot washing and mutual aid can make a difference in the ways we members of the academy as well as the church "engage" scripture.

This no doubt happens in many Anabaptist congregations. Indeed, Yoder and other Anabaptist theologians—who have tended to rely upon variant forms of Zwinglian theology of the sacraments—may fail to take into account the ways Mennonite communities of faith have in fact *formed* their children and adults for faithful living. Some of these practices are subtle, such as the communal spirituality displayed in singing hymns like "What Is This Place" in four-part harmony. Others are more overt such as the telling of the stories of the martyrs of the sixteenth and seventeenth centuries as recounted in *Martyrs Mirror* or the giving of "positive peace witnesses" periodically whether or not war is in the air.

Indeed, the very practices of reading scripture through "resourceful selectivity" and reading history by "looping back" are formed in relation to a particular kind of remembering—that kind most closely associated with the anamnesis found in the practices of foot washing and the Eucharist. As the above passage indicates, Yoder did not believe that a

Christian theological ethicist should operate independently of the body. But given the "unstable syntheses" of the contemporary United Methodist Church and the Mennonite Church, virtually all theological ethicists are going to find it hard to locate themselves solely in the bloodstream of the Body.

Rethinking Yoder's Conception of Language

Yoder and I often argued about how he responded to questions about "How to Read the Bible." Yoder had little use for hermeneutical theories as such. He preferred to describe the way he interpreted the Bible as "biblical realism."[38] I have always believed that more was going on at the level of hermeneutical theory than Yoder would acknowledge. I argued that particular ecclesial practices provided the context for the applicability of Anabaptist hermeneutics. In the more than ten years that we corresponded about these matters, Yoder was never persuaded, and I was never convinced. Our ongoing, significant argument had everything to do with the traditions within which we stood, and beyond which we continued to engage each other's writings.

In the fall of 1997, Yoder and I were in the midst of an ongoing exchange of e-mail messages about a question I had raised with him about a series of comments that he had made in his recent contribution to the Moltmann festschrift. There, in the context of a commentary on the significance of the warnings in James 3:1ff. about the destructive capabilities of language, Yoder wrote: "Language as such, attending intensely to defining terms and using language games on each other . . . is the threat."[39] I can remember stumbling over that statement because it seemed odd that John Howard Yoder—the polyglot who was so committed to the "translatability" of the gospel "for the nations" across time and cultures—would say such a thing. However, after I had given the matter further thought this statement struck me as being fully consistent with virtually everything that Yoder had written about Anabaptist hermeneutics. It reflected his own version of the Anabaptist emphasis on the (unmediated) "Inner Word" as well as his modified "Zwinglian" understanding of the sacraments.

Not coincidentally, the context of these remarks is Yoder's evenhanded but clear critique of the limits of the "moderate reformation" of British and continental forms of pietism, including the practices of John Wesley and the Methodists.[40] "In ever new incarnations," he wrote, "the Constantinian ethos accredits and co-opts the critics, thereby updating a hope correlated with socioeconomic flourishing more than with crossbearing and servanthood, and leaving most of the Gentiles outside."[41] Against such dangers, Yoder contended, "The task of theology must then be the vocation of linguistic criticism, disciplining discourse by testing its aptness for its object, and refusing any definition game that would rule out (or rule over) any part of the heritage."[42]

Yoder was very consistent about these matters during his lifetime. For example, in his 1968 essay "On the Meaning of Christmas," he warned against the syncretistic tendencies of Christmas as practiced by American Christians: "for the sake of the real meaning of incarnation we must, like the Gospels, see the cross behind the cradle. It is because that can no longer be done with the American Christmas that the time may well have come for surgery."[43] The reference to the "pruning metaphor" is by no means coincidental; it is but another example of what Yoder would later describe as reading history and tradition by "looping back." The primary difference between this piece and his later books and essays is that here Yoder is more caustic.[44]

The first time that I read this essay, I wondered how John and his family celebrated Christmas, but I never asked him that question. Having called attention to the patterns of syncretism, the author might have directed readers to ways of celebrating the birth of the Messiah that would be more productive for Christian discipleship. However, Yoder does not do so there, nor—with only a few exceptions scattered in unpublished writings across the years—does he address questions of Christian education. Even then, he typically stressed what he called a "kerygmatic philosophy of education" combined with "a philosophy of servanthood," both of which are enabled by "the corrective of discipleship."[45]

Here too, Yoder was consistent. In his last book, *For the Nations*, Yoder continued to present the role of the believing community as having the vocation of *galuth*—that is, living in exile among the dispersed peoples of the world. This Jeremianic vision of the community in exile is the setting within which the Jewish synagogue came into being. Yoder regards the advent of the synagogue to be "the most fundamental sociological innovation in the history of religions," and Yoder's understanding of the church is explicitly related to the "culture" of the synagogue.[46] There are to be no priests and no hierarchy and no orally transmitted mysteries revealed to the initiated. One only needs a canon of scriptures and a minimum number of families for "local cell of the worldwide people of God" to come into being.[47] By analogy, the vocation of the church as people of God is to "seek the peace of the city" (Jer. 29:7 KJV) in the awareness that the social shape of their community is itself the proclamation of the Gospel.

In the end, however, I find that Yoder's conception of the "shalom" of God's kingdom, vividly social as it is, nevertheless remains rather cerebral insofar as reconciliation is not mediated by anything other than social process. Yoder's account does not do justice to what happens when God troubles the waters enough to create something new out of the chaos that we have managed to make on this earth. I embrace Yoder's conception of the community-in-exile, but I can imagine such communities existing or thriving only if they are nurtured by ordinary means of grace, such as the sacraments of foot washing and the Eucharist through which disciples are formed and community is shaped as God knits lives together. While it would be wrong to say that Yoder's conception of "sacrament as social process" was narrowly Zwinglian, it would also be a mistake to ignore the ways in which Yoder's account of sacraments remained elaborately Zwinglian and radically synchronic.

Reclaiming Anabaptism as a "Means of Grace" in Post-Denominational Era

Despite my partial disagreements with Yoder and many other Anabaptists about hermeneutics and the sacraments, I nevertheless give thanks to God for the ways my life has been graced over the years by a variety of friendships with Menno's people. I count these friendships as a real "means of grace" in my life, precisely because I have been privileged to share in the kind of "holy conversation" that has nurtured my soul, lifted my spirit and redirected my path of Christian discipleship. The paradox is that I tend to place value on these relationships in ways that appear somewhat alien to the Anabaptist tradition. Namely, these have been encounters in which I have experienced the presence of God in ways as mysterious as each time I share in the celebration of the Eucharist among the people called United Methodists.

Nevertheless, Mennonites and Methodists continue to find ways to "share the house" in the midst of our disagreements about how to regard the furnishings. One area of commonality between Methodists and Mennonites is that, at our best, we are both people of God who love to sing. I especially enjoy four-part a cappella harmony and the balanced way in which the community comes to life in singing hymns like "What Is This Place." However different we may be, we surely *share* the house of God in the sense that we are attempting to respond to God's call that we be the *ekklesia*—the called-out people. My life has continued to be blessed as I join with Mennonite friends in worship from time to time while continuing to serve actively in the United Methodist Church. I also know that contemporary Mennonites struggle with many of the same issues that vex Methodists. We are all still learning to read the Bible together, and at our best we help one another see the Kingdom of God more clearly, and thereby follow Christ faithfully.

Four years ago Shalom Mennonite Church took over the building formerly occupied by Immanuel United Methodist Church in Indianapolis. The people at Shalom are still trying to come to terms with how to arrange the furnishings of this modern building that was designed for Methodist worship in the 1960s with its split chancel, console organ, vaulted roof and stained glass windows. I have found it fascinating and occasionally a bit amusing to see how these latter-day Mennos have worked through the many issues involved in the rearrangement of the furnishings of the church, particularly its sanctuary. The split chancel and choir loft is not used except for storage. The organ, which is operable, is not used because it is not needed. Most of the time the congregation sings a cappella. After four years the congregation still has not decided how they will ultimately use this space. They probably will leave the stained glass windows, even though they would not have designed the building with them. Approximately one-quarter of the congregation is from non-Mennonite backgrounds, including a retired United Methodist pastor and his wife who share in the worship and leadership of Shalom Church.

The story that has unfolded at Shalom is an apt metaphor for what it means for Methodists and Mennonites (and others) to "share the house" of the church. The situation of this congregation also reminds us of how Christians of various denominations not only find ourselves living in a post-denominational era but also in the midst of intersecting cultures in the wider world.

Rethinking Church as Culture and Place

One of Yoder's most significant contributions to contemporary theology and ethics was to call attention to the monolithic conception of "culture" deployed in such books as H. Richard Niebuhr's *Christ and Culture*. Niebuhr's typology delegitimated Anabaptist theology by portraying it as "Christ against Culture." Yoder rightly called attention to a variety of overstatements and misleading uses of Niebuhr's typology.[48] Over the past decade a growing number of Protestant theologians have offered new arguments that extend and sharpen Yoder's counterargument by rethinking the way the category of culture is used in ecclesiology and ethics.

As Phil Kenneson has recently explained, "Most of us . . . dwell in the midst of a number of cultures at any one time":

> Because the boundaries of cultures are rarely delineated sharply, we often find ourselves moving among groups of people with quite different sets of convictions, practices, institutions and narratives. We do not, however, find ourselves equally at ease in all of them. This usually goes back to matters of expectations. The cultures where I feel most "at home" are normally the ones where I best understand what is expected of me and what I can expect of other people. This is one of the reasons that many college students find it so threatening to leave the safe confines of academic life and enter the so-called real world.[49]

As Kenneson also points out, "Academic culture is not the only kind of culture that attempts to squeeze people into its mold. Because all cultures do this to some degree, the question is never simply whether we are being molded, but more importantly, into whose image are we being shaped."[50] Rodney Clapp has also argued that the church itself can be regarded as "culture in the sense that culture is a 'signifying system,' a collection of language and other signs that make sense of the otherwise chaotic and unrelated events of our lives. Culture in this regard includes 'formal and conscious beliefs'. . . but also rituals, folkways and practices, as well as feelings, attitudes and assumptions."[51]

I would like to think that the contributions of Clapp, Kenneson, et al. provide a new context for engaging the Anabaptist tradition of theology and ethics. To some extent, Yoder was a bit hamstrung. If he, as an Anabaptist theologian, discussed Mennonite community of faith as being a distinct "culture," then he found himself back in the old conceptual trap of the church-sect debate. Paradoxically, as one of the theologians who has done the most in twentieth-century theology and ethics to "break down the walls" between traditions, Yoder was also the person who always found himself in the position of needing to play the role of guest in the house, as "church" was defined by others.

But as those who have read Yoder's work carefully know all too well, he used the word "church" very carefully to designate that "shared fidelity to which believers are called,"[52] thereby reminding fellow theological ethicists that we should never attempt to domesticate God with word games. And it is precisely in that sense that I once argued that "it is not possible to disengage Yoder's practice of ecumenical dialogue from his vision of the church." Because Yoder believed that Christians share something precious—the *oikon tou theou* (house of God)—he continued to do theology out of the conviction that "fraternal admonition is the logical prerequisite for engaging in ecumenical dialogue."[53] I would like to think that such admonition can be a "means of grace" not only for the sake of repentance and restoration of community, but even more fundamentally for the regathering of the whole house of God. Such regathering is an eschatological hope, but if Yoder is right, then it must also take place within human history as well as at the end of time.

We must, therefore, keep "crossing over" to engage one another across the boundaries of denominations and traditions while at the same time engaging in the ongoing arguments that have emerged within the Christian traditions. It is my privilege to share in the worship of the congregation at Shalom Mennonite Church. On one occasion I have even offered a sermon in that company of the faithful. I also have been known to request that they sing "What Is This Place," that very evocative hymn that must have deep associations for those who sing it, despite the fact that the words appear to *deny* the significance of the memories of walls, windows and floors of houses that the lyrics of the hymn evoke.

My point in noting the paradoxical quality of the words of

the hymn, is not to call attention to this apparent contradiction in Anabaptist piety, but rather to suggest the ways in which Anabaptists—despite their Zwinglian leanings about language and sacraments—share this circumstance with Christians of other traditions. In the midst of various forms of mediation—some visual, some oral, some conveyed through other senses—congregations gather in space and time in the awareness of the diverse ties that bind them to one another (i.e., ethnicity, a heritage of hymnody, the memory of the martyrs) as well as set them apart from various others, both Christians and non-Christians. These dynamics of memory and hope interact with respect to the flesh and blood realities of congregations that in all their particularity embody the church as "treasure in earthen vessels."

The "place" referred to in Oosterhuis' great hymn is the gathered community—not the building and not the great tradition that exists across time.[54] But this is precisely the rub. I believe that the church that is gathered by God in time is also the church that exists across time and cultures. There is a passing on of the tradition that was passed on to us, and Christians are formed as well as converted—whether we believe in sacraments or not. To the extent that Mennonite congregations cannot acknowledge traditions being passed down and lives being formed through practices, they reveal a blindside in Anabaptist theology and ethics.

One of the aporias of Christian ecclesiology in our time is that some of the Christian traditions that have the most substantial theologies of the sacraments also have impoverished practices of sacramental piety. Other congregations do not have a satisfactory way of explaining to themselves the theological significance of what they do when they gather for worship. Nevertheless, to an outsider, what such congregations do in such gatherings may very well appear to be suffused with the Spirit of God, as if all the means at their disposal have become outward and visible signs of inward and spiritual grace. As Stanley Hauerwas is fond of saying, in order for United Methodist congregations to be able to baptize infants, they need to develop the disciplines that are associated with Anabaptist tradition. Similarly, I believe that Mennonites need the Eucharist in order to be able to persevere in "dying and living" as "each other's bread and wine."

Postscript: Engaging Scripture from Generation to Generation in the House of God

This spring I went back to Arkansas briefly to revisit the communities in the Ozarks where my father pastored churches and where I learned to read and began my formation as a disciple of Jesus Christ. I spent a day in Mountain View, where I visited Miriam Miller, my playmate of 35 years ago. John and Miriam both now live in Stone County. Actually, they have lived in various places over the years. John's family moved to Oregon about the same time that my family moved away in 1967, but ten years ago John moved back to Stone County. Miriam taught in South Carolina and Virginia for a while before she moved back to Mountain View.

The Baptist and the Mennonite congregations in the rural community of Richwood now have their own buildings, and the Mennonites no longer seem to have fewer cars than the Baptists and Methodists do. Miriam works in the Stone County library, where she expresses her love for books by helping children discover the wonder of reading. The old stone building containing our third grade classroom is no longer a public school; it has been converted into a church by a congregation of Pentecostals. The building that once was used to teach home economics to high school girls now houses St. Mary's Catholic Church, a small parish currently raising money in the hope of someday building its own sanctuary.

I doubt that I will ever live in Arkansas again, but I also know better than to assume that my life has not been shaped, positively and negatively, by having grown up in town and country churches where vestiges of the "religion of the lost cause" could be found in the worship practices as well as in the conversation on the front porch following revival meetings. In fact, the origins of groups like the "Royal

Ambassadors for Christ" lie in the efforts of Southern Baptists after the Civil War to create a moral culture out of the political defeat of the War Between the States. Such are the metaphors within which our identities are shaped. Human beings may seek to use such metaphors for idolatrous purposes, but God can still re-shape our souls as we learn what it means to read "in communion" with other struggling disciples who help us to learn to be accountable to the gospel that calls us to be transformed by the power of the Holy Spirit.

Today I am blessed to have Mennonite friends who care enough to lovingly tease me for the odd ways in which I often cross denominational lines in my writing about ecclesiology, racial reconciliation, and what it means to learn to read scripture well in the context of Christian practices. Among these friends are John H. Yoder's daughter Martha, who, with her husband, Rod Maust, and their four children, lives in Indianapolis. Occasionally, members of the Maust family show up for a watchnight service at the downtown United Methodist Church, where my wife is a member of the pastoral staff; and the four Cartwright progeny have been known on occasion to worship with the congregation of Shalom Mennonite Church, where John H. Yoder's grandchildren are learning what it means to be faithful disciples of Jesus Christ.

This past Christmas, the Cartwrights got together with Rod and Martha Yoder Maust and their children to sing Christmas carols. We used the old red Mennonite hymnals, and of course we sang *a cappella*, Rod and Martha patiently enduring our attempts to learn favorite Mennonite hymns while the two sets of four children noisily played throughout the house. After the families parted, it occurred to me that my children and the grandchildren of John Howard Yoder have the privilege of learning to read the Bible in a world that is much less segregated by religious affiliation than the one in which I was raised. I cannot fathom the opportunities and challenges of discipleship that the generation of Jamie Cartwright and Ruth Maust will face. The "house of faith" that they will inhabit will no doubt produce its own puzzling problems in the midst of living in various cultures at the same time.

I suspect that Jamie and Ruth's generation will not resolve such questions without engaging in some "looping back" in the interest of pruning the vine, but I believe that can only happen if they are encouraged to cultivate habits of reading and hearing the Word of God in our time. Nevertheless, I am encouraged by what is already happening. Recently, Jamie turned eight years old—the same age that I was when I first met John and Miriam. Jamie is already asking theological questions—some of which are rather startling for his mother, the United Methodist pastor, and his father, the theological ethicist. Most recently he came home from Sunday school and posed a series of questions for us. "Papa, was Jesus really Jewish?" "Yes, that is true, Jamie," his mother and I patiently replied. "Well, did he believe that he was the Messiah? Because if he was really Jewish and Jews don't believe that Jesus was the Christ, then how could Jesus believe that he was Christ?" our eight-year old disciple-in-formation inquired of his preacher-teacher-parents. I think that John Yoder would have enjoyed this exchange.[55]

Jamie already knows that Methodists are not the only people that claim to be Christians; his best friend Johnny is from a Catholic family that lives a few doors down. Johnny and Jamie are in the same class. Johnny recently celebrated his "first communion," which provoked questions that probably will take some time for Jamie to resolve. Johnny and Jamie and Ruth will learn to read the Bible in different dwellings than the ones Miriam and John and I found ourselves inhabiting 35 years ago, but I hope that they will some day realize the awesome privilege and breathtaking responsibility of "being each other's bread and wine" as members of the house of God. I pray that they will experience therein the delight and joy of God's shalom as made possible through Word and Sacrament.[56]

Notes

1. The Radical Road One Baptist Took

1. (Th.D. diss., Southwestern Baptist Theological Seminary, 1953).

2. James Wm. McClendon Jr. and Axel Steuer eds., *Is God God?* (Nashville: Abingdon, 1981).

3. James Wm. McClendon Jr. and Nancey Murphy, "Distinguishing Modern and Post-Modern Theologies," *Modern Theology* 5 (April, 1989).

4. James Wm. McClendon Jr., Curtis Freemen, and Rosalee Velloso, *Baptist Roots: A Reader in the Theology of a Christian People* (Valley Forge, Pa.: Judson, 1999).

5. James Wm. McClendon Jr. and James M. Smith, *Convictions: Defusing Religious Relativism* (Nashville: Abingdon, 1994).

2. Confessions of a Mennonite Camp Follower

1. To be sung as if Julie Andrews were a Mennonite.

2. Craig Haas and Steve Nolt, *The Mennonite Starter Kit: A Handy Guide for the New Mennonite* (Intercourse, Pa.: Good Books, 1993), 12.

3. "Willie Walker," which is what we called it at Yale Divinity School, was the text used in Church History classes at Yale. Since I did not want to "waste" my time taking church history, I just read the book and tested out of the course. That may explain why I failed to see the significance that Walker, or at least those who revised Walker's often used textbook, gave to the Anabaptists. Of course, "significance" may be too strong a word for a book that seemed determined to report just "the facts."

4. John's pamphlet was identified as "Work Paper No. 4." Marlin Miller wrote a "Foreword" for the 1966 version although John had written two prefaces, one from Basel, May 7, 1957, and the other from Basel, July 16, 1957. Michael Cartwright told me a story

that Al Meyer told him about Yoder having given Barth a copy of his essay on Barth. That led Barth to say to Yoder (and Al): "Oh, Mr. Yoder, you Mennonites are so bellicose." I am not sure how "Work Paper No. 4" found its way into the Yale Divinity Bookstore, but I suspect Jim Gustafson must have had something to do with that. I know Gustafson told me (perhaps at a meeting of the Society of Christian Ethics) that he was trying to get the book published in the new Abingdon Studies in Christian Ethics series under the title *Karl Barth and the Problem of War* (Nashville: Abingdon, 1970). That John's criticism of Barth was not well known may have been due to Abingdon's decision not to continue that venture.

5. John Howard Yoder, "The Otherness of the Church," *The Mennonite Quarterly Review* 35 (Oct. 1961): 286-96; *Peace Without Eschatology* (Evanston, Ill.: Concern, 1959).

6. I, of course, wanted to get this essay published but I had a difficult time getting anyone to take it. I sent it to many journals, but no one wanted it. The rejections often were less criticism of my essay and more reaction to Yoder. One critic explicitly said that Yoder represented a pre-Bultmannian attitude toward scripture. I should have realized that these rejections meant that any identification with Yoder was not going to win me friends, but I was too taken with what I was learning and naturally too cantankerous to care. I think the essay was finally published in the *Journal of Theology of South Africa*, but I have never seen a copy of it. I had given it to Jim Childress, who gave it to a colleague at Virginia who was on that journal's board. The latter must have sent it to South Africa. Following Paul Ramsey's advice "to never waste a word," I published the essay in my first collection, *Vision and Virtue: Essays in Christian Ethical Reflection*. The book is now published by Notre Dame (probably out of print), but was originally published by Fides Press in 1974.

7. Stanely Hauerwas, *In Good Company: The Church As Polis* (Notre Dame: University of Notre Dame, 1995) is my most extended set of reflections on this strange ecclesial anomaly to which God seems to have called some of us.

8. This is the main point of one of the essays John wrote before he died. It has just been published in *Pro Ecclesia* 9 (Spring 2000): 165-83.

9. I give a brief account of this in the "Introduction" to *The Peaceable Kingdom: A Primer in Christian Ethics* (Notre Dame: University of Notre Dame, 1983), xv-xxvi. When I reread the "Introduction" for this footnote, I realized that I'm going over some of the same ground I covered in the book. I apologize if I seem to be saying what I said before. It does make me wonder if I am the

best reporter of how my thinking has developed. My inability to remember dates is well known.

10. *He Came Preaching Peace* is now available through Wipf and Stock Publishers, 150 West Broadway, Eugene, Ore.

11. My book, *Unleashing the Scripture: Freeing the Bible from Captivity to America* (Nashville: Abingdon, 1993), has been misunderstood or ignored by most readers. That must be due to my inability to know how to proceed after my attack on sola scriptura in the first part of the book. What I did not and do not know how to do was make scriptural arguments in the manner of Yoder and Barth. All I could do in that book was exemplify how the words of scripture matter by providing sermonic examples. Probably few readers have thought it profitable to spend time checking my exegesis. The sermons, if read at all, are not read as my attempt to do scriptural reasoning, but rather as exemplifications of my "position." But Yoder is right in saying that theology has gone wrong when it becomes a position rather than a reading.

12. Richard Hays certainly began that work with his analysis of Yoder in *The Moral Vision of the New Testament: A Contemporary Introduction to New Testament Ethics* (San Francisco: Harper San Francisco, 1996), 239-53. Michael Cartwright's account of Yoder's scriptural practice in many ways remains unsurpassed. See Cartwright, "Practices, Politics, and Performance: Toward a Communal Hermeneutic for Christian Ethics" (Ph.D Diss., Duke U., 1988), 298-405.

13. Pilgram Marpeck, "Judgment and Decision," in *Classics of the Radical Reformation*, Walter Klassen and William Klassen eds. (Scottdale, Pa.: Herald Press, 1978), 332.

14. Yoder tried to think through these issues in his more "methodological" reflections about historiography. For example, read his "Anabaptism and History," in *The Priestly Kingdom: Social Ethics As Gospel* (Notre Dame: University of Notre Dame, 1984), 123-34.

15. Gerald Schlabach's "Deuteronomic or Constantinian: What Is the Most Basic Problem for Christian Social Ethics?" is one of the most promising developments for helping us to begin to think through the challenges that confront us. His essay appears in *The Wisdom of the Cross: Essays in Honor of John Howard Yoder*, Stanley Hauerwas, Chris Huebner, Harry Huebner, and Mark Nation, eds. (Grand Rapids: Eerdmans, 1999), 449-71. See also Ivan J. Kauffman, "Mennonite-Catholic Conversations in North America: History, Convergences, Opportunities," *The Mennonite Quarterly Review* 73 (Jan. 1999): 35-60.

16. This essay now appears in my *In Good Company: The Church as Polis* (Notre Dame: University of Notre Dame, 1995), 65-78; also relevant is my "Storytelling: A Response to 'Mennonites on Hauerwas,'" *Conrad Grebel Review* 13 (Spring 1995): 166-73.

17. For instance, my student Peter Dula, a Yankee fan, has told me that the Amish in Pennsylvania even play golf. (It would, of course, be acceptable if they played baseball!)

18. For this account of the body, see Joel Shuman, *The Body of Compassion: Ethics, Medicine, and the Church* (Boulder: Westview Press, 1999).

3. Following Christ Down Under: A New Zealand Perspective on Anabaptism

1. Since published as Christopher Marshall, *Faith as a Theme in Mark's Narrative* (Cambridge: Cambridge University, 1989).

2. As I attempt to outline in my little book, *Kingdom Come: The Kingdom of God in the Teaching of Jesus* (Auckland: Impetus Publications, 1993).

3. J. H. Yoder, "The Hermeneutics of the Anabaptists," in Willard M. Swartley, ed., *Essays on Biblical Interpretation* (Elkhart, Ind.: Institute of Mennonite Studies, 1984), 11-28.

4. Richard B. Hays, *The Moral Vision of the New Testament: A Contemporary Introduction to New Testament Ethics* (San Francisco: Harper San Francisco, 1996), 316.

5. Jürgen Moltmann, *Jesus Christ for Today's World* (London: SCM, 1994), 47.

6. Christopher Marshall, *Christ and Crime: Biblical Foundations for a Christian Perspective on Justice, Crime and Punishment* (Grand Rapids: Eerdmans, forthcoming).

7. See, for example, Miroslav Volf, *Exclusion and Embrace: A Theological Exploration of Identity, Otherness, and Reconciliation* (Nashville: Abingdon, 1996), esp. 275-306.

8. For a helpful discussion of Christian learning, see N. Wolterstorff, "Public Theology or Christian Learning?" in Miroslav Volf, ed., *A Passion for God's Reign: Theology, Christian Learning and the Christian Self* (Grand Rapids: Eerdmans, 1998), 65-87.

4. Anabaptist Science and Epistemology?

1. Proceedings of the conference are published in Robert J. Russell, Nancey Murphy and C. J. Isham, eds., *Quantum Cosmology and the Laws of Nature: Scientific Perspectives on Divine Action*

(Vatican City State: Vatican Observatory, 1993).

2. Nancey Murphy and George F. R. Ellis, *On the Moral Nature of the Universe: Theology, Cosmology, and Ethics* (Minneapolis: Augsburg Fortress, 1996).

3. James Wm. McClendon Jr., *Systematic Theology, Vol. 3: Witness* (Nashville: Abingdon, 2000).

4. See Rollin S. Armour, *Anabaptist Baptism: A Representative Study* (Scottdale, Pa.: Herald Press, 1966).

5. An accessible introduction to all these issues can be found in Nancey Murphy, *Reconciling Theology and Science: A Radical Reformation Perspective* (Kitchener, Ont.: Pandora Press, 1997). This book incorporates lectures I gave at the Canadian Mennonite Bible College in October 1996.

6. See Nancey Murphy, Brad Kallenberg, and Mark Thiessen Nation, eds. *Virtues and Practices in the Christian Tradition: Christian Ethics after MacIntyre* (Harrisburg, Pa.: Trinity Press, 1997). This work relies on MacIntyre's *After Virtue*, 2nd ed. (Notre Dame: University of Notre Dame, 1984).

7. MacIntyre's work on these issues is found in *Whose Justice? Which Rationality?* (Notre Dame: University of Notre Dame, 1988); and *Three Rival Versions of Moral Enquiry: Encyclopaedia, Genealogy, and Tradition* (Notre Dame: University of Notre Dame, 1990). See Nancey Murphy, *Anglo-American Postmodernity: Philosophical Perspectives on Science, Religion, and Ethics* (Boulder, Colo.: Westview Press, 1997), ch. 3 and 6; and "Overcoming Hume on his Own Terms," in D. Z. Phillips and Timothy Tessin, eds., *Religion and Hume's Legacy* (New York: St. Martin's Press, 1999), 206-20.

8. Christian Early, completing a dissertation on MacIntyre and philosophy of religion.

9. See H. Tristram Engelhardt Jr., ed., *Christian Epistemology in the Third Millennium* (forthcoming).

10. For an introductory account of these issues, see Warren S. Brown, Nancey Murphy and H. Newton Malony, eds., *Whatever Happened to the Soul?: Scientific and Theological Portraits of Human Nature* (Minneapolis: Fortress Press, 1998).

11. See Stephen Toulmin, *Cosmopolis: The Hidden Agenda of Modernity* (Chicago: University of Chicago, 1992).

5. Grace as Participation in the Inbreaking of the Kingdom

1. James William McClendon Jr., *Ethics* (Nashville: Abingdon, 1988).

2. Robert Rue Parsonage, ed. *Church-Related Higher Education*

(Valley Forge, Pa.: Judson Press, 1978).

3. *The Mennonite Quarterly Review* 69 (July, 1995). See also John D. Roth, ed. *Refocusing a Vision: Shaping Anabaptist Character in the 21st Century* (Goshen, Ind.: Mennonite Historical Society, 1995). This theme also emerged more recently in a June 2000 conference at Bethel (Kan.) College on "An Anabaptist Vision for the New Millennium: A Search for Identity." Presentations from that conference have since been published in *An Anabaptist Vision for the New Millennium: A Search for Identity*, James Juhnke and Dale Schrag, eds. (Kitchener, Ont.: Pandora Press, 2000).

4. I have published some of what I am suggesting in *Just Peacemaking: Transforming Initiatives for Justice and Peace* (Louisville: Westminster/John Knox Press, 1992), and am about to do more in some forthcoming articles.

5. In a carefully argued paper delivered in March of 2000 at the "Confronting the Powers" conference, Eastern Mennonite University, Willard Swartley argued persuasively that Matthew 5:39 should not be translated "do not resist evil" but "do not retaliate against evil." That indeed is how the teaching echoes throughout the New Testament, Romans 12 being only one example among many. See also Luke 6:27-36; 1 Thessalonians 5:15, 1 Peter 2:21-23 and Didache 1:4-5.

6. Ulrich Luz, *Matthew 1-7: A Continental Commentary* (Minneapolis: Fortress, 1989), 328.

7. Walter Grundmann, *Das Evangelium nach Matthäus* (Berlin: Evangelische Verlagsanstalt, 1968).

8. W. D. Davies and Dale C. Allison Jr., *A Critical and Exegetical Commentary on The Gospel According to Saint Matthew* (Edinburgh: T & T Clark, Ltd., 1988), 1:546.

9. I tell of this in "A Visit to East German Churches: Schooling for Democracy," *The Christian Century* (December 1989): 20-27; and in *Just Peacemaking: Transforming Initiatives for Justice and Peace* (Westminster/John Knox, 1992), 7-15, 20-31.

10. I tell more of this experience in Glen Stassen, D. M. Yeager, John Howard Yoder, *Authentic Transformation: A New Vision of Christ and Culture* (Nashville: Abingdon, 1996), 202ff.

11. Matthew 12:7, 11-14; 15:15-20; 23:23-26; Luz, *Matthew 1-7*, 52-3.

12. *Just Peacemaking*, 39ff.

13. Duane Friesen, *Artists, Citizens, Philosophers: Seeking the Peace of the City: An Anabaptist Theology of Culture* (Scottdale, Pa.: Herald Press, 2000), 51-2.

14. Ulrich Luz, *The Theology of the Gospel of Matthew* (Cambridge: Cambridge University, 1993), 31-3.

6. Latin America and Anabaptist Theology

1. José Míguez Bonino, *Doing Theology in a Revolutionary Situation* (Minneapolis: Augsburg Fortress, 1975), 2.

2. Ibid., 3.

3. "Revolución y ética evangélica," *Certeza*, (Cordoba, Argentina) 3 (1971): 104-10.

4. For a brief history and evaluation of the initial decade of the LATF, see Anthony Christopher Smith, "The Essentials of Missiology from the Latin American Perspective of the Fraternidad Teológica Latinoamericana," (Ph.D. Diss., Southern Baptist Theological Seminary, Louisville, Ky., 1983); more recently, a special issue of *Boletín Teológico* (1995): 3-4 dedicated to the LATF's 25th anniversary.

5. A briefly edited version of the English text of my paper appeared in Brian Griffiths, ed., *Is Revolution Change?* (Downers Grove, Ill.: InterVarsity, 1972), which also included articles by René Padilla and Alan Kreider.

6. I have found his analysis very helpful of how Mennonites have evolved in North America in John Howard Yoder, "Anabaptist Vision and Mennonite Reality," in *Consultation on Anabaptist Mennonite Theology*, A. J. Klassen, ed. (Elkhart, Ind.: Council of Mennonite Studies, 1970), 1-46.

7. C. René Padilla, ed., *El Reino de Dios y América Latina* (El Paso: Casa Bautista de Publicaciones, 1975). Besides chapters by Yoder and Escobar, the book includes chapters by Emilio A. Nuñez, René Padilla and José Míguez Bonino.

8. Franklin H. Littell, *The Origins of Sectarian Protestantism* (New York: Macmillan, 1964).

9. John Howard Yoder, *Jesús y la realidad política* (Buenos Aires: Certeza, 1985).

10. For a brief history and appraisal of the Lausanne movement, see John Stott, ed. *Making Christ Known: Historic Mission Documents from the Lausanne Movement, 1974-1989* (Grand Rapids: Eerdmans, 1996).

11. C. René Padilla, ed., *The New Face of Evangelicalism* (Downers Grove, Ill.: InterVarsity Press, 1976), 11-13.

12. See John H. Yoder, "Church Growth Issues in Theological Perspective," in *The Challenge of Church Growth. A Symposium*, Wilbert Shenk, ed. (Elkhart, Ind.: Institute of Mennonite Studies, 1973), 25-47.

13. John H. Yoder, "Violencia y no violencia," with a response by José Míguez Bonino, *Boletín Teológico* 42/43 (1991): 79-91.

14. Samuel Escobar and John Driver, *Christian Mission and Social Transformation* (Scottdale, Pa.: Herald Press, 1978).

15. Samuel Escobar, "The Search for a Missiological Christology in Latin America," in *Emerging Voices in Global Christian Theology,* William A. Dyrness, ed. (Grand Rapids: Zondervan, 1994), 199.

16. Yoder, "Anabaptist Vision and Mennonite Reality," 4.

17. *The Politics of Jesus* (Grand Rapids: Eerdmans, 1972), 5.

18. C. René Padilla, *Mission Between the Times* (Grand Rapids: Eerdmans, 1985), 142.

19. John H. Yoder, "The Apostle's Apology Revisited," in *The New Way of Jesus. Essays Presented to Howard Charles,* ed. William Klassen (Newton, Kan.: Faith & Life Press, 1980), 117.

20. Ibid.

21. Yoder, *The Politics of Jesus,* 21.

22. Ibid., 25.

23. Ibid., 190.

24. Escobar, "The Search for a Missiological Christology," 199-227.

25. Padilla, *Mission Between the Times,* 62.

26. Ibid., 79.

27. See their contribution in Wilbert R. Shenk, ed. *Exploring Church Growth* (Grand Rapids: Eerdmans, 1983).

28. Yoder, "The Apostle's Apology," 131.

29. Ibid.

30. Ibid., 133.

31. John H. Yoder, *As You Go. The Old Mission in a New Day* (Scottdale, Pa.: Herald Press, 1961), 10.

32. Andrew Walls, *The Missionary Movement in Christian History* (Maryknoll, N.Y.: Orbis, 1996), 9.

33. John H. Yoder, *The Priestly Kingdom: Social Ethics as Gospel* (Notre Dame: University of Notre Dame, 1984), 5.

34. Orlando E. Costas, *Liberating News* (Grand Rapids: Eerdmans, 1989), 49.

7. Anabaptism and Radical Christianity

1. Cf. Alan Kreider and Stuart Murray, *Coming Home: Stories of Anabaptists in Britain and Ireland* (Kitchener, Ont.: Pandora Press, 2000).

2. C. Rowland, *Radical Christianity* (Oxford: Polity Press, 1988).

3. James W. McClendon Jr., *Systematic Theology, Vol. 1: Ethics,* (Nashville: Abingdon, 1986); *Vol. 2: Doctrine* (Nashville: Abingdon, 1994).

4. C. Rowland, ed., *The Cambridge Companion to Liberation Theology* (Cambridge: Cambridge University 1999), 1.

5. From C. Boff, *Theology and Praxis* discussed in Rowland and

Corner, *Liberating Exegesis* (London: SPCK, 1990), 55. See also Tim Gorringe, "Political Readings of Scripture," in J. Barton, ed., *Cambridge Companion to Biblical Interpretation* (Cambridge: Cambridge University, 1998), 67-80; Gerald West, "The Bible and the Poor: A New Way of Doing Theology," in Rowland, *Cambridge Companion to Liberation Theology*, 129-52 and most recently G. West *The Academy of the Poor: Towards a Dialogical Reading of the Bible* (Sheffield: Sheffield Academic Press, 1999).

6. "Apocalyptic, the Poor and the Gospel of Matthew," *Journal of Theological Studies* 45 (1994): 504-18.

7. Thieleman J. van Braght, *Martyrs Mirror* (Scottdale, Pa.: Herald Press, 1950), 774-75.

8. "'Open Thy Mouth for the Dumb': A Task for the Exegete of Holy Scripture" (Inaugural Lecture as Dean Ireland's Professor of the Exegesis of Holy Scripture, May 11, 1992), *Biblical Interpretation* 1 (1993): 228-41.

9. Shem Peachey and Paul Peachey, eds., "The Answer of Some Who Are Called Anabaptists—Why They Do Not Attend the Churches: A Swiss Brethren Tract," *The Mennonite Quarterly Review* 45 (Jan. 1971): 5-32; on the wider hermeneutical implications, see Stuart Murray, *Biblical Interpretation in the Anabaptist Tradition* (Kitchener, Ont.: Pandora Press, 2000).

10. See Peter Matheson, *The Imaginative World of the Reformation* (Edinburgh: T & T Clark, 2000) and C. Arnold Snyder and Linda A. Huebert Hecht, *Profiles of Anabaptist Women: Sixteenth Century Reforming Pioneers* (Waterloo: Wilfrid Laurier U. Press, 1996).

11. "Response: Anglican Reflections," in P. Fiddes, ed., *Reflections on the Waters. Understanding God and the World Through the Baptism of Believers* (Oxford: Regent's Park College, 1996), 117-34.

12. See Alan Kreider, *The Change of Conversion and the Origin of Christendom* (Harrisburg: Trinity, 1999), Ch. 3.

13. See Alan Kreider, *Worship and Evangelism in Pre-Christendom* (Cambridge: Grove Books, 1995) and Tim Gorringe, *The Sign of Love: Reflections on the Eucharist* (London: SPCK, 1997).

14. *The Book of Revelation*, New Interpreter's Bible, vol. 12 (Nashville: Abingdon, 1998).

15. McClendon, *Ethics*.

8. Anabaptism as a Conversation Partner

1. This thesis, originally entitled "Spirit, Discipleship, Community: The Contemporary Significance of Anabaptist Hermeneutics," has recently been revised and updated and pub-

lished as Stuart Murray, *Biblical Interpretation in the Anabaptist Tradition* (Kitchener Ont.: Pandora Press, 2000).

2. A useful collection of essays on this subject is Rasiah Sugirtharajah, *Voices from the Margins* (London: SPCK, 1991).

3. This resulted in the production of a module for the Open Theological College entitled "Radical Christian Groups and Their Contemporary Significance."

4. One of these, "Urban Expression," which deploys self-financing mission teams in some of the least churched areas of London, has embraced several key Anabaptist values in its statement of core principles.

5. Two recent books are Stuart Murray, *Church Planting—Laying Foundations* (Carlisle: Paternoster Press, 1998 and Scottdale, Pa.: Herald Press, 2001) and Stuart Murray and Anne Wilkinson-Hayes, *Hope from the Margins* (Cambridge: Grove Books, 2000). See also Stuart Murray, "A Decade of Evangelism," *Anabaptism Today* 2 (Feb. 1993): 3-7; "Evangelism in the Radical Tradition," *Anabaptism Today* 4 (Oct. 1993): 4-9; "Church Planting: Anabaptist Style," *Anabaptism Today* 12 (June 1996): 7-14.

6. See Stuart Murray, *Explaining Church Discipline* (Tonbridge: Sovereign World, 1995).

7. See Stuart Murray, *Beyond Tithing* (Carlisle: Paternoster Press, 2000).

8. Sixty stories written by these Christians, together with a number of essays interpreting this emerging movement, are contained in Alan Kreider and Stuart Murray, *Coming Home: Stories of Anabaptists in Britain and Ireland* (Waterloo, Ont.: Pandora Press, 2000).

9. Three modular workbooks, written by me and Ian Randall, Director of Baptist and Anabaptist Studies in Prague, are available on *The Origins and Early History of Anabaptism, Baptist and Anabaptist Views of the Church* and *Anabaptists, Authority and the Bible.*

10. A surprising number of British Christians involved in the Anabaptist Network are from charismatic churches. See Stuart Murray, "Anabaptism as a Charismatic Movement," *Anabaptism Today* 8 (Feb. 1995): 7-11.

11. See Paul Peachey, "Answer of Some Who are Called (Ana)baptists Why They Do not Attend the Churches: A Swiss Brethren Tract," *The Mennonite Quarterly Review* 45 (Jan. 1971): 5-32.

12. Stuart Murray, "Interactive Preaching," *Evangel* 12 (Summer 1999): 53-7.

9. Meeting the Radical Reformation

1. A. Flannery, ed. Vatican Council II: The Conciliar and Post Conciliar Documents (Dublin: Dominican, 1975), 764.

2. John H. Yoder, *The Politics of Jesus: Vicit Agnus Noster* (Grand Rapids: Eerdmans 1972).

3. S. Windass, *Christianity versus Violence: A Social and Historical Study of War and Christianity* (London: S&W, 1964).

4. Ibid., 78; on "the pacifist heresy," cf. 84.

5. "All who take the Sword: The Pope on Violence," *Doctrine and Life* 30 (1979): 634-55.

6. Ibid., 648-9.

7. C. Arnold Snyder, *The Life and Thought of Michael Sattler* (Scottdale, Pa.: Herald Press, 1984).

8. "Michael Sattler, Benedictine and Anabaptist," *The Downside Review* 105 (1987): 111-31.

9. There are also statements in the Schleitheim Confession on the Eucharist, the ban and the oath. What is said on the Lord's Supper, however, is very interesting but not specific to the Anabaptists since Catholics have some dispute on the Eucharist with almost every other denomination.

10. "Adversus hostilem tyrannidem, quia lanceam non liceret, stilum vibrarem"; *Patrologia Latina* 182:921. "Against the tyranny of the enemy I will wield the pen, since I am not allowed to wield the sword."

11. Flannery, Vatican II, 612.

12. See U. Ó Maidín, *The Celtic Monk: Rules and Writings of Early Irish Monks* (Kalamazoo, Mich.: Cistercian, 1996).

13. Well expounded by Alan Kreider, "The Religious Teaching of Cyprian's School," in *The Change of Conversion and the Origin of Christendom* (Harrisburg: Trinity, 1999): 29-32.

14. J. Liechty, "Repentance and Hope of Peace in Ireland," *Doctrine and Life* 44 (1994): 67-74; response from a Catholic, Anglican and Presbyterian, "Corporate Repentance and Hope for Peace," ibid., 579-88.

15. Texts in M. Hurley, *Christian Unity: An Ecumenical Second Spring?* (Dublin: Veritas, 1998): 65-7; quotations from Liechty, "Repentance and Hope," 60, 73.

16. "Memory and Reconciliation: The Church and the Faults of the Past," *L' Osservatore Romano*, English edition, March 15, 2000, VI.

17. "Catholic-Mennonite Dialogue: Common Confession of the Apostle's Creed," ibid, March 8, 2000, 10.

18. See the appreciation by Kreider, *Change of Conversion*, 104-5.

19. Flannery, Vatican II (Dublin 1982), 2:29, 31.

20. Ibid., 104. E. Ferguson, "Inscriptions and the Origin of Infant Baptism," *Journal of Theological Studies*, N.S. 30 (1979): 37-46.

21. "St. Bernard, Thomas Merton, and Catholic Teaching on Peace," *Word and Spirit: A Monastic Review* 12 (1990): 54-79.

22. Roland H. Bainton, *Christian Attitudes to War and Peace* (Nashville: Abingdon, 1961).

23. *The Challenge of Peace: God's Promise and Our Response* (London: CTS, 1983).

24. *L'Osservatore Romano*, English edition, Sept. 19, 1983 (emphasis in original).

25. "Coscienza cristiana e guerra moderna," *La Civiltà Cattolica* 111 (1991): 3-16. The article did not carry the name of an author, but the thought and method are clearly that of the Pope, who had the help of some theologians with the historical section.

10. Reflections on My Encounter with the Anabaptist-Mennonite Tradition

1. Herman Hoeksema, *The Protestant Reformed Churches in America: Their Origin, Early History and Doctrine* (Grand Rapids: First Protestant Reformed Church, 1936), 16.

2. Cf. Philip Schaff, ed., *The Creeds of Christendom, with a History and Critical Notes* (Grand Rapids: Baker Books, 1996), 3:432-3.

3. Abraham Kuyper, *Lectures on Calvinism* (Grand Rapids: Eerdmans, 1931), 71-2.

4. Richard J. Mouw, *Politics and the Biblical Drama* (Grand Rapids: Eerdmans, 1996).

5. John H. Yoder, "Reformed Versus Anabaptist Social Strategies: An Inadequate Typology" and Richard J. Mouw, "Abandoning the Typology: A Reformed Assist," *TSF Bulletin* 8 (May-June 1985): 2-10.

6. Cf. Willem Balke, *Calvin and the Anabaptist Radicals*, trans. William Heynen (Grand Rapids: Eerdmans, 1981).

7. Leonard Verduin, *Honor Your Mother: Christian Reformed Church Roots in the 1834 Separation* (Grand Rapids: CRC Publications, 1988), 21.

8. Cf. F. Ernest Stoeffler's now-classic account of Dutch Reformed pietist thought in chapter 3 of his *The Rise of Evangelical Pietism* (Leiden: E. J. Brill, 1965). For an account of how the tensions between these two understandings of the church were played out in a specific dispute within Dutch Calvinist church life, see Willem van't Spijker, "Catholicity of the Church in the Secession (1834) and the Doleantie (1886)," in Paul Schrotenboer, ed., *Catholicity and Secession: A Dilemma?* (Kampen: J. H. Kok, 1992), 82-9.

11. *Embodying the Gospel in Community*

1. For an account of life at Reba Place in the early 1970s, see Dave and Neta Jackson, *Living Together in a World Falling Apart* (Carol Stream, Ill.: Creation House, 1974). For a more extended history, see Dave and Neta Jackson, *Glimpses of Glory: Thirty Years of Community. The Story of Reba Place Fellowship* (Elgin, Ill.: Brethren Press, 1987).

2. John Howard Yoder, *The Politics of Jesus* (Grand Rapids: Eerdmans, 1972).

3. Ibid., 230.

4. In rereading my old copy of *The Politics of Jesus* in preparation for this essay, I was intrigued to discover that back in 1975 I had highlighted note 9 on page 226: "In general the New Testament word *pistis* would better not be translated 'faith,' with the concentration that word has for modern man upon either a belief *content* or the *act* of believing; 'faithfulness' would generally be a more accurate rendering of its meaning." Although I had forgotten encountering this suggestion in Yoder by the time I got around to writing my doctoral dissertation, it was undoubtedly one of the seeds that germinated in my decision to explore the meaning of *pistis Iesou Christou* in Paul. See R. B. Hays, *The Faith of Jesus Christ: An Investigation of the Narrative Substructure of Galatians 3:1-4:11* (Chico, Calif.: Scholars, 1983).

5. Along the way, I was pleased to discover that Yoder had begun his academic career by writing studies of the sixteenth-century Anabaptists. See, e.g., J. H. Yoder, *Täufertum und Reformation in der Schweiz*, Bd. 1: *Die Gespräche zwischen Täufern und Reformatoren, 1523-1538* (Karlsruhe: H. Schneider, 1962) and, *Täufertum und Reformation im Gespräch: Dogmengeschichtliche Untersuchung der frühen Gespräche zwischen Schweizerischen Täufern und Reformatoren* (Zürich: EVZ-Verlag, 1968). I also learned for the first time about *The Mennonite Quarterly Review* and the modern scholarly recovery of the story of evangelical Anabaptism, and I read Harold Bender, *The Anabaptist Vision* (Scottdale, Pa.: Herald Press, 1944).

6. C. Grebel, letter to Thomas Müntzer, in G. H. Williams, ed., *Spiritual and Anabaptist Writers* (Louisville: Westminster/John Knox, 1957), 75-6.

7. See my book, *The Moral Vision of the New Testament: Community, Cross, New Creation* (San Francisco: Harper San Francisco, 1996).

12. Anabaptism and the Obstacles That Make for Vocation

1. See Rodney Clapp, "What Would Pope Stanley Say? An Interview with Stanley Hauerwas," *Books and Culture* (Nov.-Dec., 1998): 16-18; Schlabach quoted on p. 18.

13. Sharing the House of God

1. All four of our children have been baptized as infants. Here, I recall with great fondness a conversation I once had with Marlin Jeschke in the cafeteria at Goshen College during the "Rule of Christ" conference on The Concept of the Believers' Church. Jeschke expressed shock that someone as serious about church discipline as I was would also want to defend infant baptism.

2. Reflecting a longstanding medieval tradition, Huldrich Zwingli compared baptism to the monk's cowl (uniform), given upon entering the order as a novice. See William H. Willimon's discussion of Zwingli's image of the monk's cowl in *Remember Who You Are: Baptism—A Model for the Christian Life* (Nashville: The Upper Room, 1980), 92.

3. Stanza 1 of "What Is This Place," Hymn #1 in *Hymnal: A Worship Book* (Scottdale, Pa.: Herald Press, 1992). The text of this hymn, "Zomaar een dak boven wat hoofden," was written by Huub Oosterhuis (1968), and translated by David Smith (c. 1970). Although written by a Roman Catholic, this hymn has profoundly Anabaptist resonances. The prominent placement of the song as the first hymn in the hymnal is a good indicator of how evocative it is for contemporary Anabaptists.

4. Stone County was officially a "dry" county but it was well known for bootlegging.

5. For a very illuminating discussion of the complexity of memory as reconstruction and identity-forming, see John Kotre's fascinating book, *White Gloves: How We Construct Ourselves Through Memory* (New York: Norton, 1996).

6. Later I would read Walter Klasssen's book *Neither Protestant Nor Catholic* (Waterloo: Conrad Press, 1973) and discover those senses in which the perception is and is not true.

7. Stanza 2 of "What Is This Place."

8. John Howard Yoder, *The Priestly Kingdom: Social Ethics as Gospel* (Notre Dame: University of Notre Dame, 1984), 30.

9. John Howard Yoder, *The Royal Priesthood: Essays Ecclesiological and Ecumenical* (Grand Rapids: Eerdmans, 1994), 74.

10. Although the question of a "communal hermeneutic" had

been raised in different ways by such Mennonite scholars and church leaders as J. Lawrence Burkholder and William Klassen, Yoder was the only Anabaptist theologian who has to my knowledge provided the conceptual resources for making the kind of case that I wanted to make for "ecclesial hermeneutics."

11. William Klassen, *Covenant and Community: The Life, Writings, and Hermeneutics of Pilgram Marpeck* (Grand Rapids: Eerdmans, 1968). Primary sources by Pilgram Marpeck have been collected in *The Writings of Pilgram Marpeck*, trans. and ed. William Klassen and Walter Klaassen (Scottdale, Pa.: Herald Press, 1978).

12. Yoder, *The Priestly Kingdom*, 69-70.

13. Ibid., 365-6.

14. Ibid., 69-70.

15. Ibid,. 69 n. 4.

16. For a summary of Yoder's understanding of Zwingli's views, see *The Priestly Kingdom*, 69.

17. John Howard Yoder, *Body Politics: Five Practices of the Christian Community Before the Watching World* (Scottdale, Pa.: Herald Press, 2001), 27.

18. St. Bernard says that "feet represent the yearnings and desires of the soul . . . the sacrament of the washing of the feet" signifies forgiveness with regard to all our daily sins.—St. Bernard, "Sermon for Holy Thursday," cited in Jean Vanier, *The Scandal of Service: Jesus Washes Our Feet* (Toronto: Novalis/Continuum, 1998), 40.

19. Yoder, *The Royal Priesthood*, 13.

20. My thinking about the significance of foot washing has been shaped by the writings and ministry of Jean Vanier. See in particular Vanier's *The Scandal of Service*, 38-41.

21. See the diagram in my Editorial Introduction to *The Royal Priesthood*, 13.

22. *The Priestly Kingdom*, 31-2.

23. Ibid., 101. I am grateful to Gerald Schlabach of the University of St. Thomas for calling this passage to my attention.

24. There is no record that Yoder specifically objected to the use of the phrase "means of grace" in interpretive projects to which he contributed where the context made it clear that "cultic worship is not an end in itself." For example, see Millard Lind's eight proposals to guide the practice of Christian worship discussed in Ross Bender's, *The People of God: A Mennonite Interpretation of the Free Church Tradition* (Scottdale, Pa.: Herald Press, 1971), 143.

25. *The Priestly Kingdom*, 43.

26. Yoder's pieces "On the Meaning of Christmas" and his "Marginalia—The Case Against Christmas" in *Concern* No. 16

(November 1968): 14-9, 19-22 offer the most notable instance of Yoder's elaborately Zwinglian critique, but it is surely not the only example to be found.

27. Stanza 3 of "What Is This Place."

28. Donald F. Durnbaugh, *The Believers' Church: The History and Character of Radical Protestantism* (Scottdale, Pa.: Herald Press, 1968; rpt. 1985), 130-45. See also Franklin Littell's classic study, *The Free Church: The Significance of the Left Wing of the Reformation for Modern American Protestantism* (Boston: Starr King Press, 1957).

29. Albert Outler made this observation in his prefatory remarks about John Wesley's sermon "Of the Church" (1785), Sermon 74 in *The Works of John Wesley* (Nashville: Abingdon Press, 1986), 46. According to Outler, "The essence of the church, for Wesley, need not be sought in its visible institutions, not even some invisible numerus electorum. The church as the Body of Christ is the company of all true believers, 'holy' because its members are themselves holy." Outler regarded this same sermon as the founder of Methodism's "most mature ecclesiological reflection," a judgment with which I agree. I also concur with Outler's judgment that the historical and ecumenical significance of Wesley's "unstable" synthesis has not received the attention that it deserves.

30. For an illuminating discussion of this ecumenical vocation, see the essay "Ecclesial Location and Ecumenical Vocation" in Geoffrey Wainwright, *The Ecumenical Moment: Crisis and Opportunity for the Church* (Grand Rapids: Eerdmans, 1983), 196-9.

31. See Yoder's letter to Dennis Stoesz, archivist at the Archives of the Mennonite Church, Goshen College, offering an explanation of the context of another paper, "Christian Education: Doctrinal Orientation," that he prepared in the late 1950s in the context of a debate about "whether it was possible or desirable to try to get a network of church-administered high schools, so that most young people whose parents were committed Mennonite Christians would not send their young people to public schools." As Yoder's letter explains, the paper was prepared with a view toward "beginning a conversation which it was hoped would become an issue of the *Concern* pamphlet series. Responses were promised, but never came, from people active in developing the church-high school movement and from other perspectives. The issue never came out, and the question died down when it became obvious that for purely financial reasons church-governed high school education would remain a minority privilege whether we liked it or not."

32. John Howard Yoder, "To Serve Our God and Rule the World," originally published in *The Annual of the Society of Christian Ethics*, 1988, republished in *The Royal Priesthood: Essays Ecclesiological and*

Ecumenical (Grand Rapids: Eerdmans, 1994), 128-40.

33. Ibid., 139.

34. Ibid., 139-40.

35. Ibid., 140.

36. In a conversation with Gerald Schlabach at the University of Notre Dame, liturgical scholar Mark Searle once remarked that there was a sense in which "the Amish and the Cistercians have much more in common with each other than either of us [as Mennonites or Catholics] have with them."

37. Stephen Fowl, *Engaging Scripture: A Model for Theological Interpretation* (Oxford: Blackwell, 1998), 175.

38. I was asked to review the manuscript of his collection of essays on "How to Be Read by the Bible," and I recommended that it not be published because Yoder did not engage the contemporary debate in any significant way and he had not adequately explained "biblical realism." Subsequently these essays have been made available through Wipf & Stock publishers. Yoder thought my interest in hermeneutical theory, both in my dissertation and subsequent essays, was an incipient form of what he often described as "methodologism."

39. John H. Yoder, "Is There Such a Thing as Being Ready for Another Millennium?" in *The Future of Theology: Essays in Honor of Jürgen Moltmann*, Volf, Krieg, and Kershary, eds. (Grand Rapids: Eerdmans, 1996), 68.

40. In my judgment, Yoder always did have his finger on most if not all of the internal contradictions of pietism, whether expressed in Methodist or Mennonite dress.

41. Yoder, "Is There Such a Thing as Being Ready for Another Millennium?" 67.

42. Ibid., 68. Yoder included an explanatory footnote where he spelled out the connection between his argument in this context about the role of the "academic theologian" and the role of the "monarchical pastorate." Clearly, Yoder saw what he was writing here as fully consistent with the position he had developed in *The Fullness of Christ* (1986) and other essays about the apostle Paul's "vision of universal ministry."

43. John H. Yoder, "On the Meaning of Christmas," *Concern*, 16 (Nov. 1968): 18-19.

44. The piece is set alongside a caustic poem "Nasty Noel," in which Yoder, writing under the pen name of "Henderson Nylrod," satirizes the practice of Christmas gift-giving.

45. John H. Yoder, "A Syllabus of Issues Facing the Church College," a lecture presented at the three Mennonite colleges prior to a workshop convened by the Mennonite Board of Education

(April 1964): 18, 20-1.

46. John Howard Yoder, *For the Nations: Essays Public and Evangelical* (Grand Rapids: Eerdmans, 1997), 71.

47. Ibid., 72.

48. John Howard Yoder, "How H. Richard Niebuhr Reasoned: A Critique of Christ and Culture," in *Authentic Transformation: A New Vision of Christ and Culture*, Glen H. Stassen, D. M. Yeager and John Howard Yoder, eds. (Nashville: Abingdon, 1996), 31-89.

49. Philip Kenneson, *Life on the Vine: Cultivating the Fruit of the Spirit in Christian Community* (Downers Grove, Ill.: InterVarsity, 1999), 25.

50. Ibid.

51. Rodney Clapp, *A Peculiar People: The Church as Culture in a Post-Modern Society* (Downers Grove, Ill.: InterVarsity, 1996), 173-4.

52. Yoder, "How H. Richard Niebuhr Reasons," *Authentic Transformation*, 281, n. 101.

53. Michael G. Cartwright, "Radical Reform, Radical Catholicity: John Howard Yoder's Vision of the Faithful Church," *The Royal Priesthood*, 1.

54. Yoder came by his radically synchronic account of the church honestly. As Mark Nation has recently argued, Yoder's approach to ecumenicity is that of a "Neo-Anabaptist" in the best sense of the word. See Nation's Ph.D. dissertation "The Ecumenical Patience and Vocation of John Howard Yoder: A Study in Theological Ethics" (Fuller Seminary, 2000).

55. Yoder wrote a series of essays collected as "The Jewish-Christian Schism Revisited" (Elkhart, Ind.: Shalom Desktop packet, 1996). He believed that part of the problem that Christians in our day have to contend with is that we have allowed our traditional categories to shape our assessment of what took place during the first two centuries of early Christian history. Yoder thought contemporary Christians needed to loop back to recover aspects of our faith that have been left aside in the midst of overstated and misstated distinctions.

56. I am grateful for the comments and corrections of Martha Yoder Maust and Gerald Schlabach on an earlier draft of this essay.

Works Cited

Allison, Dale C. and W. D. Davies. *A Critical and Exegetical Commentary on the Gospel According to Saint Matthew.* Edinburgh: T & T Clark, 1988.

Armour, Rollin S. *Anabaptist Baptism: A Representative Study.* Scottdale, Pa.: Herald Press, 1966.

Bainton, Roland H. *Christian Attitudes to War and Peace.* Nashville: Abingdon, 1961.

Balke, William. *Calvin and the Anabaptist Radicals.* William Heymen, trans. Grand Rapids: Eerdmans, 1981.

Barton, J., ed. *Cambridge Companion to Biblical Interpretation.* Cambridge: Cambridge University, 1998.

Bender, Harold. *The Anabaptist Vision.* Scottdale, Pa.: Herald Press, 1944.

Bender, Ross. *The People of God: A Mennonite Interpretation of the Free Church Tradition.* Scottdale, Pa.: Herald Press, 1971.

Bonino, Jóse Míguez. *Doing Theology in a Revolutionary Situation.* Minneapolis: Fortress, 1975.

Clapp, Rodney. *A Peculiar People: The Church Culture in a Post-Modern Society.* Downers Grove, Ill.: InterVarsity, 1996.

Costas, Orlando E. *Liberating News.* Grand Rapids: Eerdmans, 1989.

Durnbaugh, Donald F. *The Believers' Church: The History and Character of Radical Protestantism.* Scottdale, Pa.: Herald Press, 1985.

Dyrness, William A., ed. *Emerging Voices in Global Christian Theology.* Grand Rapids: Zondervan, 1994.

Englehardt, H. Tristam Jr., ed. *Christian Epistemology in the Third Millennium.* Forthcoming.

Escobar, Samuel and John Driver. *Christian Mission and Social Transformation.* Scottdale, Pa.: Herald Press, 1978.

Fiddes, P., ed. *Reflections on the Waters: Understanding God and the World Through the Baptism of Believers.* Oxford: Regent's Park College, 1996.

Fowl, Stephen. *Engaging Scripture: A Model for Theological Interpretation.* Oxford: Blackwell, 1998.

Friesen, Duane. *Artists, Citizens, Philosophers: Seeking the Peace of the City: An Anabaptist Theology of Culture.* Scottdale, Pa.: Herald Press, 2000.

Griffiths, Brian, ed. *Is Revolution Change?* Downers Grove, Ill.: InterVarsity, 1972.

Grundmann, Walter. *Das Evangelium nach Matthëus.* Berlin: Evangelische Verlagsanstalt, 1968.

Gorringe, Tim. *The Sign of Love: Reflections on the Eucharist.* London: SPCK, 1997.

Haas, Craig and Steve Nolt. *The Mennonite Starter Kit: A Handy Guide for the Mennonite.* Intercourse, Pa.: Good Books, 1993.

Hauerwas, Stanley. *In Good Company: The Church as Polis.* Notre Dame: University of Notre Dame, 1995.

———. *The Peaceable Kingdom: A Primer in Christian Ethics.* Notre Dame: University of Notre Dame, 1983.

———. *Unleashing the Scripture: Freeing the Bible from Captivity to America.* Nashville: Abingdon, 1993.

———. *Vision and Virtue: Essays in Christian Ethical Reflection.* Fides, 1974.

———, Chris Huebner, Harry Huebner, and Mark Nation, eds. *The Wisdom of the Cross: Essays in Honor of John Howard Yoder.* Grand Rapids: Eerdmans, 1999.

Hays, Richard. *The Moral Vision of the New Testament: A Contemporary Introduction to New Testament Ethics.* San Francisco: Harper San Franciso, 1996.

——— and Luke Timothy Johnson. *The Faith of Jesus Christ: An Investigation of the Narrative Substructure of Galatians 3:1-4:11,* 2nd ed. Grand Rapids: Eerdmans, 2001.

Hoeksema, Herman. *The Protestant Reformed Churches in America: Their Origin, Early History, and Doctrine.* Grand Rapids: First Protestant Reformed Church, 1936.

Jackson, Dave and Neta. *Glimpses of Glory: Thirty Years of Community. The Story of Reba Place Fellowship.* Elgin, Ill.: Brethren Press, 1987.

———. *Living Together in a World Falling Apart.* Carol Stream, Ill.: Creation House, 1974.

Juhnke, James and Dale Schrag, eds. *An Anabaptist Vision for the New Millennium: A Search for Identity.* Kitchener, Ont.: Pandora Press, 2000.

Kenneson, Philip. *Life on the Vine: Cultivating the Fruit of the Spirit in Christian Community.* Downers Grove, Ill.: InterVarsity Press, 1999.

Klassen, A. J., ed. *Consultation on Anabaptist Mennonite Theology.* Elkhart, Ind.: Council of Mennonite Studies, 1970.

Klassen, Walter. *Anabaptism: Neither Protestant nor Catholic.* Waterloo: Conrad Press, 1973.

_____. *The Writings of Pilgram Marpeck.* Scottdale, Pa.: Herald Press, 1978.

_____ and William Klassen, eds. *Classics of the Radical Reformation.* Scottdale, Pa.: Herald Press, 1978.

Klassen, William. *Covenant and Community: The Life, Writings, and Hermeneutics of Pilgram Marpeck.* Grand Rapids: Eerdmans, 1968.

_____, ed. *The New Way of Jesus, Essays Presented to Howard Charles,* Newton, Kan.: Faith & Life Press, 1980.

Kotre, John. *White Gloves: How We Construct Ourselves Through Memory.* New York: W.W. Norton, 1996.

Kreider, Alan. *The Change of Conversion and the Origin of Christendom.* Harrisburg, Pa.: Trinity Press, 1999.

_____. *Worship and Evangelism in Pre-Christendom.* Cambridge: Grove Books, 1995.

_____ and Stuart Murray. *Coming Home: Stories of Anabaptists in Britain and Ireland.* Kitchener, Ont.: Pandora Press, 2000.

Kuyper, Abraham. *Lectures on Calvinism.* Grand Rapids: Eerdmans, 1943.

Littell, Franklin. *The Free Church: The Significance of the Left Wing of the Reformation for Modern American Protestantism.* Boston: Starr King Press, 1957.

_____. *The Origins of Sectarian Protestantism.* New York: Macmillan, 1964.

Luz, Ulrich. *Matthew 1-7: A Continental Commentary.* Minneapolis: Fortress, 1989.

_____. *The Theology and Gospel of Matthew.* Cambridge: Cambridge University, 1993.

MacIntrye, Alasdair. *After Virtue,* 2nd ed. (Notre Dame: University of Notre Dame, 1984).

_____. *Three Rival Versions of Moral Enquiry: Encyclopaedia, Genealogy, and Tradition.* Notre Dame: University of Notre Dame, 1990.

_____. *Whose Justice? Which Rationality?* Notre Dame: University of Notre Dame, 1988.

Maidin, U. O. *The Celtic Monk: Rules and Writings of Early Irish Monks.* Listercian, 1996.

Marshall, Christopher. *Christ and Crime: Biblical Foundations for a Christian Perspective on Justice, Crime, and Punishment.* Grand Rapids: Eerdmans, forthcoming.

____. *Faith as a Theme in Mark's Narrative.* Cambridge: Cambridge University, 1989.

____. *Kingdom Come: The Kingdom of God in the Teaching of Jesus.* Auckland: Impetus Publications, 1993.

Matheson, Peter. *The Imaginative World of the Reformation.* Edinburgh: T & T Clark, 2000.

McClendon, James Wm. Jr. *Systematic Theology, Vol 1: Ethics.* Nashville: Abingdon, 1986.

____. *Systematic Theology, Vol. 2: Doctrine.* Nashville: Abingdon, 1994.

____. *Systematic Theology, Vol. 3: Witness.* Nashville: Abingdon, 2000.

____ and Axel Stuer eds. *Is God God?* Nashville: Abingdon, 1981.

____, Curtis Freeman, and Rosalee Velloso eds. *Baptist Roots: A Reader in the Theology of a Christian People.* Valley Forge, Pa.: Judson, 1999.

____ and James Smith. *Convictions: Defusing Religious Relativism.* Nashville: Abingdon, 1994.

Moltmann, Jürgen. *Jesus Christ for Today's World.* London: SCM, 1994.

Mouw, Richard J. *Politics and the Biblical Drama.* Grand Rapids: Eerdmans, 1996.

Murphy, Nancey. *Anglo-American Postmodernity: Philosophical Perspectives on Science, Religion, and Ethics.* Boulder, Colo.: Westview Press, 1997.

____. *Reconciling Theology and Science: A Radical Reformation Perspective.* Kitchener, Ont.: Pandora Press, 1997.

____, Brad Kallenberg, and Mark Nation, eds. *Virtues and Practices in the Christian Tradition: Christian Ethics After McIntyre.* Harrisburg, Pa.: Trinity Press, 1997.

____ and George F. R. Ellis. *On the Moral Nature of the Universe: Theology, Cosmology, and Ethics.* Minneapolis: Fortress, 1996.

____, Robert J. Russell, and C. J. Isham, eds. *Quantum Cosmology and the Laws of Nature: Scientific Perspectives on Divine Action.* Vatican City State: Vatican Observatory, 1993.

____, William S. Brown, and Newton Malony, eds. *Whatever Happened to the Soul?: Scientific and Theological Portraits of Human Nature.* Minneapolis: Fortress, 1998.

Murray, Stuart. *Beyond Tithing.* Carlisle: Paternoster Press, 2000.

____. *Biblical Interpretation in the Anabaptist Tradition.* Kitchener, Ont.: Pandora Press, 2000.

_____. *Church Planting: Laying Foundations*. Scottdale, Pa.: Herald Press, 2001.

_____. *Explaining Church Discipline*. Tonbridge: Sovereign Word, 1995.

_____ and Anne Wilkinson-Hayes. *Hope for the Margins*. Cambridge: Grove Books, 2000.

Padilla, C. René. *Mission Between the Time*. Grand Rapids: Eerdmans, 1985.

_____, ed. *The New Face of Evangelicalism*. Downers Grove, Ill.: InterVarsity, 1976.

_____,ed. *El Reino de Dios y América Latina*. El Paso: Casa Bautistade Publicaciones, 1975.

Parsonage, Robert Rue, ed. *Church-Related Higher Education*. Valley Forge, Pa.: Judson Press, 1978.

Phillips, D. Z. and Timothy Tessin, eds. *Religion and Hume's Legacy*, New York: St. Martin's Press, 1999.

Rowland, Christopher. *The Cambridge Companion to Liberation Theology*. Cambridge: Cambridge University, 1999.

_____. *Radical Christianity*. Oxford: Polity Press, 1988.

Roth, John D., ed. *Refocusing Vision: Shaping Anabaptist Character in the 21st Century*. Goshen, Ind.: Mennonite Historical Society, 1995.

Schaff, Phillip, ed. *The Creeds of Christendom, with a History and Critical Notes*. Grand Rapids: Baker Books, 1996.

Schrotenboer, Paul, ed. *Catholicity and Secession: A Dilemma?* J. H. Kok, 1992.

Shenk, Wilbert, ed. *The Challenge of Church Growth. A Symposium*. Elkhart, Ind.: Institute of Mennonite Studies, 1973.

_____. *Exploring Church Growth*. Grand Rapids: Eerdmans, 1983.

Shuman, Joel. *The Body of Compassion: Ethics, Medicine, and the Church*. Boulder, Colo.: Westview Press, 1999.

Snyder, C. Arnold. *The Life of Michael Sattler*. Scottdale, Pa.: Herald Press, 1984.

_____ and Linda A. Hecht. *Profiles of Anabaptist Women: Sixteenth Century Reforming Pioneers*. Waterloo: Winifred Laurier University, 1996.

Stassen, Glen H. *Just Peacemaking: Transforming Initiatives for Justice and Peace*. Louisville: Westminster/John Knox, 1992.

_____, John Howard Yoder, and D.M. Yeager. *Authentic Transformation: A New Vision of Christ and Culture*. Nashville: Abingdon, 1996.

Stott, John, ed. *Making Christ Known: Historic Mission Documents from the Lusanne Movement*. Grand Rapids: Eerdmans, 1996.

Rasiah Sugirtharajah. *Voices from the Margins*. London: SPCK, 1991.

Swartley, Willard, ed. *Essays on Biblical Interpretation*. Elkhart, Ind.: Institute of Mennonite Studies, 1984.

Toulmin, Stephen. *Cosmopolis: The Hidden Agenda of Modernity*, Chicago: University of Chicago, 1992.

van Braght, Theileman J. *Martyrs Mirror*. Scottdale, Pa.: Herald Press, 1950.

Vanier, Jean. *The Scandal of Service: Jesus Washes Our Feet*. Toronto: Novalis/Continuum, 1998.

Verduin, Leonard. *Honor Your Mother: Christian Reformed Church Roots in the 1834 Separation*. Grand Rapids: CRC Publications, 1988.

Volf, Krieg and Kershary, eds. *The Future of Theology: Essays in Honor of Jürgen Moltmann*. Grand Rapids: Eerdmans, 1996.

Volf, Miroslav. *Exclusion and Embrace: A Theological Exploration of Identity, Otherness, and Reconciliation*. Nashville: Abingdon, 1996.

____, ed. *A Passion for God's Reign: Theology, Christian Learning, and the Christian Self*. Grand Rapids: Eerdmans, 1998.

Wainwright, Geoffrey. *The Ecumenical Moment: Crisis and Opportunity for the Church*. Grand Rapids: Eerdmans, 1983.

Walker, Williston. *A History of the Christian Church*. New York: Scribner, 1985.

Walls, Andrew. *The Missionary Movement in Christian History*. Maryknoll, New York: Orbis, 1996.

West, G. *The Academy of the Poor: Towards a Dialogical Reading of the Bible*. Sheffield, England: Sheffield Academic Press, 1999.

Williams, G. H., ed. *Spiritual and Anabaptist Writers*. Louisville: Westminster/John Knox, 1957.

Windass, S. *Christianity versus Violence: A Social and Historical Study of War and Christianity*. London: S&W, 1964.

Yoder, John Howard. *As You Go. The Old Mission in a New Day*. Scottdale, Pa.: Herald Press, 1961.

____. *Body Politics: Five Practices of Christian Community Before the Watching World*. Scottdale, Pa.: Herald Press, 2001.

____. *For the Nations: Essays Evangelical and Public*. Grand Rapids: Eerdmans, 1997.

____. *He Came Preaching Peace*. Eugene, Ore.: Wipf and Stock Publishers, 1998.

____. *The Peaceable Kingdom: A Primer in Christian Ethics*. Notre Dame: University of Notre Dame, 1983.

_____. *The Politics of Jesus: Vicit Agnus Noster*. Grand Rapids: Eerdmans, 1972.

_____. *The Priestly Kingdom: Social Ethics as Gospel*. Notre Dame: University of Notre Dame, 1984.

_____. *The Royal Priesthood: Essay Ecclesiological and Ecumenical*. Grand Rapids: Eerdmans, 1994.

Index

About
the Editor

John D. Roth is professor of history at Goshen College in Indiana where he also serves as director of the Mennonite Historical Library and editor of *The Mennonite Quarterly Review*. He and his wife Ruth are the parents of four daughters and are active members in the Berkey Avenue Mennonite Fellowship.

Herald Press Titles
by John Howard Yoder

Body Politics

Five Practices of the Christian Community Before the Watching World

Binding and loosing, baptism, eucharist, multiplicity of gifts, and open meeting; these five New Testament practices were central in the life of the early Christian community.

Yoder, in his inimitably direct and discerning style, uncovers the original meaning of the five practices and shows why the recovery of these practices is so important for the social, economic, and political witness of the church today.

Paper. 90 pages. 0-8361-9160-9: $14.99; in Canada $23.49

Christian Witness to the State

"John Yoder wrote *The Christian Witness to the State* to save Mennonites from Reinhold Niebuhr's backhanded compliment that their commitment to nonviolence is admirable as long as they recognize that they are politically irresponsible. This small book, however, is now a crucial resource for all Christians who seek to live faithful to the politics of Jesus."
—Stanley Hauerwas, Duke Divinity School
Paper. 96 pages. 0-8361-9209-5: $14.99, in Canada $23.49

Christist and the Powers

John Howard Yoder, translator.

"**Hendrik Berkhof's** important book, *Christ and the Powers*, was the fountainhead of studies on the Powers. Yoder introduced it to an English-speaking audience and used it in his own groundbreaking work. Its impact can be seen on William Stringfellow, Jacques Ellul, and any number of writers, including myself."—*Walter Wink, author of a triology on the Powers*

Paper. 80 pages. 0-8361-1820-0: $8.99; in Canada $14.29

A Declaration on Peace

In God's People the World's Renewal Has Begun

A call from Mennonites, Quakers, Church of the Brethren, and the Fellowship of Reconciliation to all Christians to renew discussions about peace, war, militarism, and justice. Edited by Douglas Gwyn, George Hunsinger, Eugene F. Roop, and John Howard Yoder.

Paper. 112 pages. 0-8361-3541-5: $5.99; in Canada $9.49

Nevertheless

The Varieties and Shortcomings of Religious Pacifism

John Howard Yoder's classic book first published in 1971, includes a treatment of Jewish pacifism, bibliographies, an index, and three new appendixes. Yoder points out assumptions, strengths, and shortcomings of each pacifist position. He brings clarity to the many-sided conversations about peace, nonviolence, war, proliferation of arms, and power politics.

Paper. 192 pages. 0-8361-3586-5: $11.99; in Canada $18.79

The Royal Priesthood

Essays Ecclesiological and Ecumenical

John Howard Yoder poses challenges for Christians of all communions by calling for disciplined dialogue and faithful servanthood that renders the confession of Jesus Christ's lordship meaningful.

Paper. 396 pages. 0-8361-9114-5: $19.99; in Canada $31.29

The Schleitheim Confession

John Howard Yoder, editor and translator. In the historic
meeting held in 1527 at Schleitheim, Switzerland, an ad hoc
group of Anabaptists worked through fundamental disagreements and emerged with a consensus on seven points
of faith that became known as the Schleitheim Confession.
One chapter from *The Legacy of Michael Sattler*.
Paper. 32 pages. 0-8361-1831-6: $2.99; in Canada $4.79

What Would You Do?

As a peace-loving Christian, what would you do if someone
attacked your grandmother, wife, daughter (or grandfather,
husband, son)? John Howard Yoder explores the pros and
cons of a nonviolent response. Viewpoints on the subject
and examples from life are included ranging from Dale
Aukerman to Leo Tolstoy, from Joan Baez to Tom Skinner.
Paper. 144 pages. 0-8361-3603-9: $7.99; in Canada $12.49